More Praise for
The Invisible Employee

An incredible book I could not put down. Managers beware, lest your star employees go from Number 1 to gone in a blink of an eye. Read and apply the lessons of this book! Or better yet, don't and I'll hire all your *stars* when they leave *you*.

> Anthony Lopez
> Managing Director
> DePuy, a Johnson & Johnson company
> Author of *The Legacy Leader* and
> *Breakthrough Thinking*

The Invisible Employee captures the essence of how great leaders use employee recognition to drive excellence. There are gems in every chapter that will help any manager build a more productive team. This is a delightful book that every manager should not only read, but study.

> Jean-Luc Butel
> President
> Medtronic Asia/Pacific

This book is a must-read for any employer who wants to keep talent motivated, inspired, and on board for years to come. *The Invisible Employee* helps managers tap into the real driver of employee motivation. Learning what motivates individuals will enable any employer to retain top talent, provide employees with personal and professional growth opportunities, and cultivate employee loyalty.

Scott Northcutt
Executive Vice President
Human Resources, DHL Americas

the invisible employee

Other Books by Adrian Gostick and Chester Elton

A Carrot a Day
The 24-Carrot Manager
Managing with Carrots

Books by Adrian Gostick and Dana Telford

The Integrity Advantage
Integrity Works

Book by Adrian Gostick, Illustrated by Shauna Raso

Daniel Sparrow: A Holiday Story

the invisible employee

Realizing the Hidden Potential in Everyone

Adrian **Gostick &**
Chester **Elton**

WILEY

JOHN WILEY & SONS, INC.

For general information on our other products and services or for
technical support, please contact our Customer Care Department
within the United States at (800) 762-2974, outside the United
States at (317) 572-3993 or fax (317) 572-4002.

Wiley also publishes its books in a variety of electronic formats.
Some content that appears in print may not be available in
electronic books. For more information about Wiley products,
visit our web site at www.wiley.com.

ISBN-13: 978-0-471-77739-7
ISBN-10: 0-471-77739-0

Printed in the United States of America.

10 9 8 7 6 5 4 3 2 1

To Kent, who has made so much possible . . .
for our careers and our families.

CONTENTS

ACKNOWLEDGMENTS

The Invisible Employee is the culmination of many people's contributions, and thanks are due to a number of people.

First, to Larry Alexander and Laurie Harting at John Wiley & Sons who so quickly saw the vision of this idea and within a week of seeing a proposal secured the book for John Wiley & Sons.

Next, to our key contacts at the companies we have quoted including Bill Newby at Xcel Energy; Ray Mageau at EPCOR; Cheryl Hutchinson at Friendly's; Rich Siegenthaler, Debbie Vorndran, and Bob Joyce at Westfield Group; Tony Treglia, Joan Kelly, Rosemary Magrone, and Scott Northcutt at DHL; and Eric Lange at VNU Media Measurement.

To our many clients from whom we have learned so much and who have graciously shared so many stories and examples with us, only a few of which could fit within these pages.

To David Jackson and Alan Acton at The Jackson Organization for your research assistance on this book and those to come. And to our valuable copyeditor and researcher, Christie Giles.

To our family at O. C. Tanner that includes Joyce Anderson, Kaye Jorgensen, John McVeigh, Kent Murdock, David Petersen, Kevin Salmon, David Sturt, and Tim Treu and their incredible teams, for their leadership and vision. We thank all those in marketing and sales (including the Beasts of the East, they know who they are), and all those we've neglected, for your thought-leadership in the world of recognition and rewards.

To our amazing Carrot team of B. J. Beckman, Max Brown, Scott Christopher, Cordell Clinger, Mindi Cox, Bob Ann Hall, Angie Haugen, Chad Johnson, Ann Norman, Shauna Raso, Richard Sheinaus, Amy Skylling, and Wylie Thomas.

And as always, we must thank our families: to Jennifer and Tony, and to Heidi, Cassi, Carter, Brinden, and Garrett. We have spent countless days away developing these ideas, and we thank you for your patience, love, support . . . and laughs.

It is not possible to create a list like this and remember everyone. To those who read these acknowledgments and feel left out . . . invisible if you will . . . please feel free to write and let us know and we'll send a humble apology.

Finally, to all the good bosses out there, thank you, thank you, thank you for bringing your employees out of the shadows. To all the good bosses we've had, thanks for your great example. And to those lousy ones? Well, we appreciate the comic material you provided us.

INTRODUCTION

One of my [Adrian's] favorite photographs of my
parents was taken in the 1950s. My dad is on a
ramshackle Norton 500 motorbike and my
mother is seated next to him in a sidecar. On her
lap is their Border collie, Puccini. On the pillion
behind my father is strapped a bulky canvas tent
and a suitcase.

They were taking a vacation—before the kids arrived—camping on the English coast. A quick escape from my dad's job at Rolls-Royce. Riding in their first, rather modest vehicle.

When I saw the photo a few years ago, I smiled and teased my dad, "They didn't pay you very well at Rolls, did they?"

He chuckled and told me the story of joining Rolls-Royce in Derby, England, as a very young draftsman of jet airplane components. He agreed that the company never did pay exorbitant wages. In fact, 25 years later, he would finally leave England for Canada and triple his salary. And while he did receive numerous promotions along the way, I'm also afraid Rolls-Royce couldn't offer Gordon Gostick growth into senior leadership—since there was a bottleneck of older talent ahead of him. Still, he did he stay there more than two decades. Why?

My dad explained, "You know, I enjoyed every day. You weren't just a number going to work at Royce's. Managers actually talked to you and listened to what you had to say. When we identified a problem coming up in taking an engine concept to manufacturing, those above you in your department—and in other departments—would accept the knowledge you'd built up in your certain area, and they'd modify the design to improve the final engine. Everybody had their input."

When asked what happened when an improvement idea came from him, he said simply, "My name was on the drawing."

What a simple formula. When he spoke, someone listened. When he did something remarkable that furthered the company's progress, his name was on the drawing that went up to management. And that meant that every day he actually enjoyed going into work—now that is a big deal.

Wouldn't it be great if your company was filled with employees like Gordon Gostick—people who were excited to go in to work? Not full of employees who mumble a sad prayer on the train, "Dear Lord, please strike me down before I get there." Or worse yet, "Please bless that my boss died over the weekend in a freak gardening accident."

In his book, *Achieving Total Quality*, Wayne H. Brunetti writes that the greatest reward you can offer employees is actually listening to their ideas and acknowledging their contribution. "The most important thing to keep in mind is that employees want management to implement the team's solution if the solution solves the problem. This is the highest form of recognition. Credit must be given when credit is due."

Now, as you know, not everyone is missing the boat on this. There are some great companies to work for. There is a reason people will wait for months and months just to get an interview with Southwest Airlines. In fact, it's more competitive to get hired by Southwest Airlines for $10 an hour as a baggage handler than to be accepted into the Harvard School of Business. Only 4 percent of the 90,000 people who apply for work at Southwest each year are actually hired. Now that is unbelievable. Can you imagine your kid coming to you after high school saying, "Mom, Dad, I think I know what I want to do with my life. I want to be a gate attendant for Southwest." And you are forced to crush the dream: "Whoa, there junior. You may be setting your sights too high. Why don't you apply to Harvard instead?"

That's the power of an affirming culture. It is rare. And people will stand in line to work there. In the interim, most of us settle for places like those described by a study quoted in the *New York Times*, where:

- 25 percent of employees reported being driven to tears in the workplace.
- 50 percent call their place of work a place of "verbal abuse" and "yelling."
- 30 percent are regularly given unrealistic deadlines.
- 52 percent have to work 12-hour days to get the work done.
- One in 12 complain their chair hurts their posterior.

The sad thing is most leaders of people have no idea about the unhealthy state of their workplaces. They have a pretty darn clear idea what their bosses want. They know quite a bit about their customers and their needs. They can recite by heart their product lists. But what do they really know about the needs of the people who actually get the work done for them? Hmmm . . . not so much.

And why is that important? Because, quite simply, employees work harder for people who care about them as individuals—don't you? Think about it for a moment. Whom do *you* work harder to please: the boss who is aloof and inattentive, focused on furthering his career, or the leader who is actively interested in your work achievements and asks about your kids and your weekend fishing passion? The old adage "I don't care if they like me as long as they respect me," is not only wrong, it's dangerous in the modern workplace.

And it's a leadership attitude that's causing more than a few problems with our workforce. One problem is called presenteeism. Now absenteeism is easy to spot, but presenteeism describes workers who show up every day, but who really aren't there. They are present, but are limited by physical or mental issues, obsessed with problems at home, or, most often, overly concerned with on-the-job difficulties. Too many of these folks are burned out, stressed, underutilized, or simply ignored by their leaders. The *Harvard Business Review* estimates presenteeism costs American businesses $150 billion annually in direct and indirect costs.

Here's more sobering news about our managerial effectiveness. According to several recent studies, as much as 30 percent of the average workforce is "actively disengaged." That means up to 3 out of 10 people in your workplace are not only uncaring about their jobs, the quality of their work, or giving you their best ideas and energy, but are actively recruiting others to join them in their discontent.

And the word on the street is that it's not going to get better any time soon. According to a 2003 survey, 90 percent of workers say they want their leaders to notice their efforts and improve their recognition and rewards before they will feel committed to their organizations.

In short, we could write a book about the epidemic of invisible employees and the chaos they leave in their wake. And, actually we have.

We began this book a few years ago, after the release of our "Carrot" series of business books. Many of those who read the books asked us to speak in their organizations and we found ourselves meeting leaders and line managers from a variety of industries in countries around the world.

At first blush, every single one of the managers we met looked great. They all wore spiffy, professional clothes, had the right vocabulary and flawless posture, and knew their industries and its jargon. But the real revelation of their competence came when we spoke to the *employees* working for them. For the most part, the people who worked for great bosses were confident and outgoing. They seemed to be able to do anything and weren't afraid of change or competition. These employees seemed to revel in giving their best work and best ideas to further the goals of the organization.

But we also met a group of employees who were very different. Some of these folks were quieter and more reserved, others were obsessed with frightening market conditions that threatened their futures. In the worst cases, some were openly contemptuous. They complained about their needy customers, their coworkers, and, especially, their bosses.

These employees worked for lousy bosses— and they spent their days quietly undermining the efforts of their teams, managers, and companies. Some were actively cynical. Why? Because they lived in the shadows, rarely noticed.

They were . . . invisible.

We wish we could say we didn't understand how they felt. But, personally, we've worked for good managers and some lousy managers ourselves. And the difference is dramatic. So when we thought of all the people suffering through pitiful bosses in this world, and of all the managers who want to be good bosses but just don't know how, or don't have the time or the tools, we knew we had to write this book.

So here it is. The pages that follow contain the stories of leaders who have learned how to manage employees in ways that make those people feel valued and appreciated. The key word here is *learned*. Because most of us have to work at recognizing and appreciating others. Our natural instinct tells us to look out for number one and to keep other people down. But the best managers have committed to *learning* the art of recognition and appreciation. And it's well worth the effort. In the end, seeing—and rewarding—employees for their efforts pays off in ways nothing else can:

- As a strategic force. (You reward behaviors you want repeated.)
- As a superior communication methodology. (No one tunes out when a peer is being recognized.)
- By creating an emotional bond between employees and managers. (When's the last time a company newsletter had that kind of impact?)
- By making managers and employees better. (When you get an award, you can't help feeling more committed and filled with a stronger sense of purpose.)
- By impacting your bottom line. (People who feel appreciated, do what they do better.)

In today's competitive environment, all of us are looking for the next big product, the next big capability or solution. And a workforce of visible, committed, caring employees (if you have them) is the only way to achieve those results.

Look for inspiration in the project spreadsheet or strategy document or any other place and chances are, you'll miss it entirely. A wise investment of your time in seeing and rewarding your employees is an investment in the continued success of your company. It's an investment that truly appreciates.

You can bank on that.

And so, as you begin, our hope is that *The Invisible Employee* will be a profit finder in your organization—guiding you in the secrets of engaging the people you already have to enhance the strength of your organization. As you will find in the coming pages, recognizing and engaging people is not the soft side of business. It is the very basis of business success . . . and of success in life in general, when you really think about it. Everyone needs to be recognized and appreciated—from the CEO of a worldwide corporation to a kindergarten child.

I [Chester] will always remember the unhappy, moody child I noticed at the elementary school while waiting to pick up my own son. His caregiver (maybe his mom) was listening half-heartedly to the teacher, who was saying what an improved day the obviously challenging boy had had, and was trying to outline some of the specific, positive things the boy had done. Finally, cutting the teacher off, the woman nodded and said, flippantly, "Oh, well, isn't that just great. See you tomorrow."

The child's face fell and he shook his head while the woman dragged him off.

Contrast that with Sandy Simon, a team leader at Xcel Energy in Denver, when we spoke to her a few months ago. She had just been one of several winners of the company's highest achievement, the Pinnacle Award.

"All I could think about when I was stepping off the stage was, 'What am I going to do to get back here next year?'" she said.

That's an employee who is on fire. That's an employee who will make a difference for her company this year and next. And all because her contributions were seen and rewarded.

So our hope is simple: That you will find the invisible employees in your organization or team and bring them out of the shadows—realizing their full potential. For us, this book is a manifesto of the unseen and unrecognized, dedicated to all those people who work hard and achieve so much every day. By seeing and recognizing their accomplishments, we know you will build stronger teams and companies.

And you'll find, *seeing* is achieving. Every time. Everywhere. With everyone.

the
invisible
employee

CHAPTER ONE

Invisible
People

Invisible People. That's what the Highlanders of the island called the mysterious beings who filled their vaults with treasures—but were rarely ever seen.

On special occasions, in candlelit halls, the elders sometimes gathered the Highlanders together. In low voices, they repeated the legend of how the Invisible People had once lived openly among them; but had slowly faded into the background until they were mere hints of the men and women they had once been.

"Yet, they live among us still..." the storyteller would say, looking vaguely past the flickering lights. "They are a part of us. It is they who scale the mountains for the valuable jewels. It is they for whom we leave the Fruits of the Laborer."

A thrill would run up the Highlanders' backs. Many would glance nervously at the shadows of chairs and children and water jugs dancing around the edges of the room. But the Highlanders' eyes, dimmed by generations of disuse, saw nothing more.

Always at this point, a child would innocently ask in a high voice, "Doesn't anyone ever see them now?"

"Never." The elder would say firmly. "It is the way."

And around the room, all would breathe a collective sigh of relief. It was good to know that tomorrow things would go on as they always had on their island in the Medeokr Sea. Invisible hands would do the work. The Highlanders would go on seeing what they always saw, missing what they always missed. All would be in order. And that was enough for them. . . .

And what of the Invisible People? At their own meeting, high in the mountain foothills, the Wurc-Ur tribe, as they called themselves, huddled together, the fire crackling and popping.

"You want to be safe," an older tribeswoman said to the young. "You want to be comfortable. If you don't want to experience failure and criticism and exhaustion, then you must perfect the art of silence. The art of invisibility."

Another elder nodded and added, "It has become our only refuge."

Young Star, a tall graceful Wurc-Ur, could recite the next part by heart. Silently, her lips mouthed the story of the days when the Highlanders had earned their name by scaling the mounains themselves.

The gems were so plentiful then that the Highlanders had brought thousands of Wurc-Urs to the island to help harvest them. In time, the Wurc-Urs became so skilled that the Highlanders rarely ventured up the mountain themselves, preferring instead to remain at the base, where the water flowed cold and pure and the trees grew tall and strong.

Still, they kept the name of Highlanders, as a denotation of their high status on the island—for they controlled the mountains with their riches and the lowland orchards with their jewel-toned fruit.

"We brought down many rubies—and even diamonds—in those days," the elder of the Wurc-Urs would remember. "Before...before that terrible time."

Yes. That terrible time, thought Star, when the Highlanders eliminated many hundreds of Wurc-Urs. The few remaining tribespeople worked harder and harder, but their efforts rarely met with approval. Finally, they retreated into the shadows of the mountains, their spirits beaten. Star had been a baby at the time. But her father had been there. He knew.

She vowed never to let the same thing happen again.

And so Star learned not to stand out. Not to display her strengths. Not to do more than was necessary. Like everyone else, she learned to blend in. It was an art. She and others learned it young and learned it well.

Or at least, most Wurc-Urs did. Once, just a few years before, an innovative and committed tribesman had traveled to the top of one of the mountains, where glittering diamonds littered the crevasses. Few Wurc-Urs had ever made it to that height. The journey was treacherous, tiring...and lonely. But he had done it—and brought back a bag bulging with the rare glittering stones. The Highlanders had received them greedily. And for a brief time afterward, Wurc-Ur motivation to reach the summit was rekindled. But their extra efforts were greeted with silence from the Highlanders—as if diamonds of this quality were to be expected. And eventually the Wurc-Urs abandoned plans for new journeys to the top. Their quiet lives soon returned to normal. After all, why should they risk so much for so little?

I will never find a diamond. Or even an emerald, thought Star. It was more a statement of fact, or maybe even an oath, than an expression of regret, for she had never really wanted to climb to such heights. No one did.

And so, in this way, the dim-sighted Highlanders and the unremarkable Wurc-Urs managed to live side-by-side for generations on mountainous Kopani Island. Safe, but forever stagnant. No heroes. No villains. And they liked it that way.

Or so they thought....

INVISIBLE EMPLOYEES

Why Employees Feel Invisible

It can happen to anyone . . . anytime . . . anywhere. You're hunched over the speaker during a conference call, straining to hear, or picking up a fax, and *wham!* Suddenly, you're invisible.

Like most people, Allison never saw it coming. Working in the public relations department of a prominent national bank, one of her assignments was to write the cost-of-living report for the corporate economist. It took a fair amount of time. She met with the economist a couple times each month to prepare for the press conference and to review the report. Things were going well until one day . . .

"I was walking down the hall and overheard him [the economist] talking to my boss. He said, 'Could you get this over to the *girl* who does the cost-of-living report?' The *girl*? It was like someone had punched me in the stomach. We'd worked together for more than a year. I'd improved the quality of the report and the media reach. I'd spent hundreds of hours on his project, met with him at least twice a month. And he *didn't even remember my name.*"

Wham! Inexplicably, unbelievably, Allison suddenly found herself *invisible.*

"He didn't see me as a person. I was just a cog in the machinery. It was an eye-opening experience for me."

Sadly, Allison isn't the only one feeling invisible these days. Some 88 percent of employees surveyed say their biggest beef with their organization is "not enough acknowledgment of their work," says Adele B. Lynn of Lynn Learning Labs. That's not a few malcontents, but a remarkable 9 out of 10 workers who feel unappreciated.

Here's another frightening stat: *Time* magazine reported in February 2005 that 80 percent of employees believe they get no respect at work. That kind of disrespect can break your heart, literally. Just listen to this: In a study of health care workers, employees working for a boss they disliked had higher blood pressure than those who liked their bosses. Which, according to British scientist George Fieldman, could increase the risk of coronary heart disease by one-sixth and the risk of stroke by one-third.

We say in jest that a bad manager is "killing me." In reality, they just may be.

Invisible Employees Do Unremarkable Work

In your employees' perspective, managers and senior leaders hold all the power. Management decides when they come and go, what they work on, how much they get paid, what their dental plan looks like, when they take vacation, when they get yelled at, and when they are smiled upon. And, if the company does particularly well, it's management that gets almost all the rewards.

Feeling overlooked, ignored, and unappreciated, invisible employees fight back the only way they know how . . . by staying hidden in the corporate shadows, doing just enough to get by, grumbling about this and that . . . and passing these techniques along to new hires.

After all, they reason, why bother shining when no one notices your above-and-beyond achievements? Why bother trying when you could be in the next batch of layoffs?

David Sirota, coauthor of *The Enthusiastic Employee,* sees it all too often. "About 16 percent of the companies we deal with have a hostile workforce," he says. "But the bulk of the problem is not hostility. It is that people have become indifferent. That is the silent killer."

The Global Employee Commitment Study by Hewitt Associates has quantified the problem: As high as 54 percent of the workforce within lower-performing companies is made up of disengaged employees and people who place themselves or their careers over company needs. Backing that up is a survey of 5,000 households by The Conference Board, which found that two out of three workers do not feel motivated to drive their employer's business goals.

In other words, it's a thankless job . . . and employees are not about to do it. Or, at least, not very well.

An Engaging Solution

It's not that way for everyone, however. Some leaders engage their people in their cause and find a way to bring out their best. How do they do it?

Not with more money, although for many, that's their first resort. Hit employees with a quick shot to the pocketbook to keep them or make them happy. But although a paycheck (even a fat one) will get people to show up at work, it never bought long-term commitment.

Said Marcus Buckingham and Curt Coffman in their book *First, Break All the Rules,* "If you are paying 20 percent below the market average, then you may have difficulty attracting people. But bringing your pay and benefits package up to market levels, while a sensible first step, will not take you very far. These kinds of issues are like tickets to the ballpark—they can get you into the game, but they can't help you win."

No, the best managers move their teams and companies from ordinary to extraordinary by something as simple as:

- *Setting* a guiding vision
- Actively *seeing* employee achievements that move your organization toward its goals
- *Celebrating* those achievements

Great leaders, you see, lead people—not systems, processes, technology, strategy, or functions. Because, when it comes right down to it, all those things can be replicated—but your people can't.

Ruben Roman is a young, brawny plant manager at the Comanche Plant of Xcel Energy in Colorado. He knows recognition isn't the soft side of business. In fact, he knows the company's recognition program, Xpress Ideas, which rewards employees for innovative ideas and solutions, generated more than $15 million in savings to the company over the past year.

In one case in Roman's plant, a sealed air blower used to create a positive air system around the coal feeders went out in the middle of the night. The coal dust in the air created a dangerous environment for workers. Since there was no spare blower or redundant system, it looked like they would have to take the unit offline until a replacement blower could be brought in two days later.

"But Xcel Energy employees, any time they hear a problem, are looking for a solution," said Roman. "So they figured out a way to attach air hoses to pressurized air headers so we didn't have to take the unit offline."

Roman estimates the cost of losing power for those two days would have totaled about half a million dollars. And if his employees were disengaged, that's probably just what would have happened. Instead, the employees came up with a creative idea. And what did Roman do? The very next day he presented them with tangible recognition awards, costing a few hundred dollars, and the employees were thrilled with the public recognition of their accomplishment.

Over time, ideas like that add up.

"Recognition absolutely encourages ideas," says Roman. "You see someone with an iPOD and they tell you it's from recognition. Suddenly, everyone has a lot of ideas—about things people have been tolerating for years because that's the way it's always been. . . . It's good for companies to have these programs because otherwise the ideas just stay out there in people's heads."

Of course, the impact of company strategy, products, and technology cannot be overlooked. But neither can a company live by a spreadsheet alone. Successful companies have to have that *something extra* to create staying power. And that something extra is the passion of your people who feel noticed, valued, and appreciated. In other words, they feel *visible.*

In the Gallup organization's ongoing survey of more than four million employees worldwide, there is a remarkable evidence of the business impact of recognition and praise. In a supporting analysis of 10,000 businesses units within 30 industries, Gallup found that employees who are recognized regularly:

- Increase their individual productivity
- Increase engagement among their colleagues
- Are more likely to stay with their organization

- Receive higher loyalty and satisfaction scores from customers
- Have better safety records and fewer accidents on the job

Not too shabby. And it just makes sense. How else do you build a global company like DHL with their worldwide on-time delivery, or The Men's Wearhouse where everyone will treat you as nicely as the bearded owner in the commercials, or Edward Jones, which for two years in a row was named No. 1 in *Fortune's* "100 Best Places to Work" list?

The answer is: You can't . . . without a committed, engaged workforce.

To achieve your goals of profitability, growth, client satisfaction, or innovation, you have to have employees who care. They have to commit. They have to feel good about what they are doing. They must be able to trust that company leadership will listen to and recognize their accomplishments.

And their ability to do all that hinges on the ability of a leader to do those three simple leadership steps we mentioned earlier. In other words, they:

1. **Set** guiding core values for their team or company—values that they believe will bring greater productivity, profitability, and market share.

2. **See** employee behaviors that support the core values and create value.

3. **Celebrate** those behaviors in a public manner through recognition—communicating what activities are most important to their organization and encouraging their repetition.

And when a leader does these things, he or she is destined to succeed.

Kent Murdock, CEO of the O. C. Tanner Recognition Company, used the process this way: During a companywide meeting that kicked off a daunting computer overhaul that he knew would tax the entire organization, he asked every one of the 2,000 employees for their personal help. It was one of the most human, moving speeches we've heard.

He said, "I'll tell you how we're going to save this company. . . . I don't know. But if human ingenuity can bring about a miracle, or something smaller than that, then we're going to do it. And I will do everything in my power to accomplish this. But my power doesn't include all the ideas or all the work or all the working together that we need. My brain doesn't contain all the answers, but I'll know a good one when I hear it. And I'll recognize that person for it. Our future is in your heads collectively. Together, we can be Albert Einstein. We can be geniuses. What do you say, can we do it?"

He then opened his door, walked the halls, and he listened.

And ideas started coming in. Tentatively at first. But when he recognized the good ones in public celebrations, they started *pouring* in. And the result? In the three years since that speech—by better noticing and recognizing employee efforts—his 75-year-old company has grown more than 20 percent in sales while actually reducing headcount through attrition.

It's a simple formula, but one that eludes most managers.

And perhaps some confusion is understandable. We have, after all, been laboring for years under a flawed management mind-set. Conventional wisdom says that increasing customer, investor, and employee loyalties are three different and distinct business objectives. We extrapolated that to believe they were mutually exclusive.

As a result, during the 1990s and early 2000s, as our collective mind-set turned to shareholders, we turned away from employees.

It was a terrible, terrible time.

Even today, almost every senior executive (90 percent, according to a recent investigation) say that people are their company's greatest asset, and a full 98 percent declare that increasing productivity would enhance the bottom line. But that's where it stops; it's just talk. Given the chance to rank the strategies most likely to bring success, executives put the people issues—performance and investment in the workforce—near the bottom.

As a result, an astounding 65 percent of Americans reported receiving no recognition for good work in the past year. Not only that, half of managers agree that they do not recognize or reward their employees for performance. And nearly 75 percent of managers do not see a need for a companywide systematic approach to managing employee performance.

In response, workers have created another statistic: Only 14 percent report being very satisfied with their jobs, according to a 2005 survey by The Conference Board. Less than stellar engagement, to say the least. Actually, less than *abysmal* engagement, to tell you the truth.

So what can we do about it? That's next.

SURVEYS: AN EYE-OPENING EXPERIENCE

Is your hair standing on end? We wouldn't be surprised if it was. We've been quoting some pretty scary numbers on employee satisfaction. On the other hand, you may feel your team or your company has much less dissatisfaction than the 40 percent to 50 percent we have suggested can occur—and we certainly hope you are right.

Either way, it's good to know for sure. And an employee survey will tell you exactly what kind of company you are keeping.

But beware: Surveys can be tricky. We were recently in one of the largest companies in the world after a workplace satisfaction study had been conducted. The leaders of this multibillion-dollar concern were thrilled to find the survey showed just single-digit dissatisfaction in their ranks. But when we spoke with workers, we heard of some creative test prep from middle managers around the world. Said one employee in a phone center in the western United States, "Our boss announced an across-the-board twenty-five cent an hour raise right before the survey." Said an employee in Canada, "We were warned by our division director that centers that scored low in the past had been closed."

Perhaps not the most unbiased data.

To really find out what percentage of your employees are disengaged, carefully conduct your research with an outside firm if possible and listen to their advice on test taking—whether to use a census or a survey, which questions to include, what response rates are acceptable, and so on. There are many wonderful organizations that do this kind of research. And we've put a few examples of survey questions on our web site at **invisibleemployee.com**. When you get there, click on Surveys.

Now, if you have a smaller organization or you lead a team and want your own results, there's nothing to say you can't do this on your own. However, the lack of anonymity might keep many of your employees from responding openly to a formal survey. A simple tactic is to conduct personal, one-on-one interviews in your closed office. Turn off the phone, put a do-not-disturb sign on the door, and use the following open-ended questions:

- From your perspective, what are the most important goals of our team/organization?

- Other than an income to pay your bills, what motivates you to do this job well and live the values of our team?

- What are some of the things that might be keeping you from realizing your full potential or realizing our team goals?

- As a manager, how should I be helping you achieve these goals?

- Do you think we celebrate enough the successes of our team, and your personal achievements?

By using these simple questions, as well as others you develop, it is possible to extrapolate a fairly accurate picture of your workplace. Most importantly, the mere act of measuring or inquiring about employee satisfaction has its own benefits. It shows you care. And that is always a good place to start.

VISIBLE TOOL

Quiz: You're an Invisible Employee If . . .

1. You have only the foggiest idea what the formal goals/values of your team or corporation are, and you don't really care to know.

2. It's been several years since one of your ideas was implemented by management.

3. Your boss doesn't listen to you, in fact, rarely even looks up from checking e-mail when you are in her office.

4. You haven't been recognized in the past week with specific praise from your direct supervisor.

5. It's been at least a year since you've received a tangible award in a public manner for a great accomplishment.

6. When you receive recognition, it often comes weeks or months later.

7. You can't remember the last time your manager celebrated an important team victory.

8. Everyone in your area gets the same rewards, no matter what their individual contribution is.

9. You wouldn't even dream about recommending your company to a friend.

10. At 5:01 P.M., every day, you are on your way home.

Score

If you agreed with:

1 or 2 answers	You may be an invisible employee.
3 to 8 answers	You *are* an invisible employee.
9 or 10 answers	You are about to blink out.

CHAPTER TWO

Blink Outs

"Tell me again why we do this?" Star called out breathlessly to the man walking several steps ahead of her. Jon laughed as he moved quickly and effortlessly up the mountain.

"Do you like to eat?" he joked, not even breathing hard.

"Maybe I could learn to live without food," muttered Star, as she cut a wide berth around a sleepy snake sunning on a rock. And she wasn't alone in her opinion. These days, most Wurc-Urs found climbing not just mundane, but maddening. The thankless monotony of scorching days on the trail; the threat of being seen by Highlanders monitoring the hillside from below—it was a constant balancing

19

act between the effort needed to get the job done and the restraint necessary to avoid drawing attention. She and the other Wurc-Urs spent a good part of their day complaining to each other and hiding from the Highlanders. Not that they were really watching much anymore, but you could never be too careful.

Stopping in the shade of a small tree, Star looked up at Jon. "Hey, you ready for a break?" she said.

Jon winked and turned back to join her. He had the athletic build of the Wurc-Urs, with pale translucent skin and hair. It would take a sharp-eyed Highlander to spot him, thought Star. That is, if they ever cared to look.

"I don't know how he blends in so well," Star mumbled with respect. It was no secret that Jon was one of the most skilled climbers among the Wurc-Urs. He had once reached the elevation where precious diamonds could be found. But when she asked him about it, he had just shrugged.

The bags they carried now were empty. They gathered jewels on the way down, not up. That was one secret Jon had taught her about to conserve energy. Another was to throw the filled bags down steep inclines instead of carrying them down. Sure, it broke a few stones, but it made the downhill trip much more comfortable. It was one of the many ways they'd learned to cut corners—making their jobs easier.

"Hey, looks like they're getting ready for the Fruit of the Laborer ceremony down there," Star said, nodding at the Highlander village far below.

On the new moon and the half moon, the High-landers made the journey to offering spots on the foothills of each mountain. There, they col-lected the chests of jewels from the Wurc-Urs and left the Fruits of the Laborer, baskets of fruits, grains, and vegetables that made up the Wurc-Urs staple diet. Purple and blue, crimson and gold, the exotic fruits picked from Highlander orchards would glisten in the moonlight almost as brightly as the jewels.

Star's mouth watered, thinking of the warm, sweet fruit.

Star knew that besides being payment for the jewels, the offering was a bribe—to continue bring-ing down the gems. And usually, it worked. Although the piles of jewels never grew in size or quality, they did continue to be brought down by the bagful year after year... despite the risks. After all, the Wurc-Urs did need to eat. And the Highlanders had dominion not only of the mountains, but also of the fields that grew the only food on the island.

But lately, something had been happening. Some-thing that disrupted the flow of life on Kopani. Try as she might, Star had never been able get close enough to hear what the old timers whispered as they stood close together at the edge of the evening fires, their brows wrinkled in worry.

But Jon had.

"Have you heard what the others are saying?" he asked as he glided up beside Star.

She shook her head and leaned in, conspiratorially.

"Blink Outs. That's what's happening." Star noticed that his pride in revealing this made him slightly more visible for the moment.

"Wurc-Urs just disappear," he snapped his fingers. "Like that. Into thin air. The elders don't know why it's happening. Or how to stop it."

A scared look crossed his face. "Four Wurc-Urs have disappeared just this week."

So that's what it was. Blink Outs. Could it be true? Star thought about it as she walked the trail. Her mind flashed through faces of dear friends she might lose. She thought about the unique skills of each of the climbers that might be lost—how Saria always knew where to find deep gorges with the hidden gems, how others were expert climbers who trained the young. What if they lost Remi, who could foretell when mountain conditions were unsafe? She even caught herself selfishly thinking about all the extra trips up the mountain she would have to make if more of her people Blinked Out.

∞

And then it was time for the ceremony.

It was a spectacular night: Clear and warm, with a patchwork of bright stars in the heavens.

Star was standing on the edge of the clearing, watching the Highlanders dance in their elaborate attire. In a long procession they swirled and pirouetted, their orange banners trailing and catching the starlight—like a red-hot stick removed from the fire and waved in the night air.

Star was standing near Jon, when she heard him muse, softly, half-wonderingly, "They really don't care where the gems come from as long as they're here. They might as well just fall from the heavens."

On most days, Star would not have disagreed. But on this day it was hard to criticize the Highlanders as they made their offering to the Wurc-Urs. "But they are dancing for us," said Star.

Jon smiled as a father would to a misguided child. "Perhaps once they danced for us, but not anymore. They dance because it makes the gems come. They don't dance for us. No one cares about us anymore. Now, they dance for themselves."

Star thought about that for a moment and shrugged. This wasn't the night for this discussion.

"Oh, never mind all of that," she said. "It's a beautiful night and—"

It happened in an instant. As Star turned her head to tease Jon out of his melancholy, she heard a soft pop! And suddenly, shockingly, Jon wasn't there. Not invisible. Not faded gently into the background. Gone. In a blink.

And in his place was only a profound silence.

BLINK OUTS

Why Workers Leave

What if we told you that one thing was to blame 79 percent of the time when people leave? Would you do something about it? Well, according to the Society of Human Resource Management, 79 percent of people who leave their jobs do so because of a *lack of recognition or appreciation.*

Not surprisingly, Prudential Financial came up with similar results when they sponsored a companywide project aimed at collecting information from current and former employees, as well as future candidates. "Not feeling valued and appreciated for the job they did" was one of the top reasons former employees gave for leaving the company.

In a day and age where workers are asked to do more with less, they are rebelling. Not by holding up picket signs outside your factory gate. But by grumbling, finding ways to cut corners and, eventually, blinking out.

What's *love* got to do with work? A lot, it appears, when it comes to employee satisfaction.

People Don't Leave for Money . . . They Often Leave Supervisors

While most managers we've interviewed seem to be convinced it's the twice-monthly paycheck that buys them the commitment of their people, surprisingly money is rarely at the top of employee lists of work satisfiers. While a paycheck gets them to show up every day, it doesn't buy long-term engagement. And maybe that's not so surprising, when you really think about it.

Consider how much more money employees make when they leave your company. An employee may say, "They're doubling my wages!" Yeah, right. How about "I'm getting 50 percent more." Probably not. Sure, some people might be leaving for a genuinely better financial situation—a 20 percent pay raise, for example. But since the average increase in salary is just 5 percent in North America, what does that tell you? Some people are actually leaving for a whole lot less money.

The truth is, some people are taking a pay cut to leave . . . *you*. Yikes.

A study by the Saratoga Institute showed that 50 percent of work satisfaction comes from an employee's relationship with his or her immediate boss. And when that relationship goes sour, well, so does the whole workplace situation. In interviews with 20,000 workers who had just left an employer, the Saratoga Institute found that their supervisors' behavior was the main reason most people quit. You might find this difficult to believe—unless it has happened to you.

We met a sharp businesswoman recently after we spoke at the International Association of Business Communicators annual meeting. She came up afterward, while we were rushing to pack up to catch a plane, and stopped us cold. She had worked in health care. "I never thought that was true before," she said, "about people leaving bosses. But it happened to me. I had a terrible boss." She actually shuddered slightly with the memory. "She was just in it for herself."

"So you blinked out?" we asked.

She nodded. "I left and found a great place to work. I have a wonderful boss who thanks me all the time."

Good for the new company. Bad for the other. Maybe even worse than they think.

The Talented Are the First to Go

You've probably read or heard how long ago, in a coal mine, a small bird would signal trouble. The miners regularly took a canary or other bird below ground as an early warning system. They knew that if deadly, invisible gases were present, the birds would be the first to react. In other words, if Tweetie dropped dead, it was time to get out.

The workplace equivalent of these canaries are your star employees. Thankfully, they don't drop dead, they just blink out.

Says Marshall Goldsmith, founding director of the Alliance for Strategic Leadership, "When high-impact performers are asked why they left an organization, many report, 'No one ever asked me to stay!' Many executives do not tell high-impact performers that they are special, for fear of alienating 'average' performers. But this practice makes it difficult to retain top performers."

Jack Welch, former CEO of General Electric, took pains to identify his firm's top performers and let them know they were making a difference. Of them he said, "The top 20 percent must be loved, nurtured, and rewarded in the soul and wallet because they are the ones who make magic happen."

But when the atmosphere at a company is poisonous—the best are usually the first to go.

So how do you stop the exodus? By improving the recognition ratio.

Think about yesterday. How many times did you offer criticism (even constructive) or correction? And how many times did you offer praise or express gratitude?

For many employees on the receiving end, the ratio isn't positive. One employee in the services industry said to us, "When I make a mistake I'm recognized 100 percent of the time; when I do something great, I'm *not* recognized 99 percent of the time."

Sobering, isn't it? One percent recognition.

But what if employees were recognized for great behavior even 2 percent of the time? Or better yet, how about 10 percent, 20 percent or even 40 percent of the time? You might be surprised what happens.

Here's what can happen in just one industry: food service.

If you've ever worked in a restaurant, you know the environment makes all the difference. Restaurants can be team-oriented places with fun coworkers, great products, and engaging bosses. Or they can places of stressful demands, challenging fellow employees, little praise, and tremendous turnover (up to 300 percent annually).

It doesn't take long when you enter a Friendly's Ice Cream restaurant to see they are creating a great work environment.

Take the restaurant in Hershey, Pennsylvania, where Beverly Gomez is the general manager. If you think you're busy trying to get to know your people, Beverly has 77 employees reporting to her. But since Gomez took over this restaurant two years ago, turnover is down 25 percent and the financials are fantastic.

What's her secret?

"You've got to be genuinely concerned about your people," she said. "You've got to treat everyone the same, but different. You watch and see what motivates each of them."

This great manager told us the story of a dishwasher in her restaurant. The employee was relatively new and a little slower than other dishwashers. Many managers wouldn't reward an "underachiever," fearing what other employees would think. Gomez is not most managers.

"Recently, she did something spectacular for her, got the dish area cleaned up in half an hour, where sometimes it might take her 45 minutes," said Gomez. "I gave her an ice cream cake to take home and in a one-on-one presentation I was specific about what she did that was great. Well, you might have thought I'd given her the world."

And the reaction from the employee? "She's more open to me. She talks to me more often. Being a general manager intimidates a lot of people. So by me rewarding her with a cake, it made her feel more comfortable around me. Today, we are much closer. In fact, when dishes start to stack, I dig in and help her."

Simple recognition of an underachiever. But recognition that has gone a long way to building a strong relationship.

Not long ago, a survey of thousands of full-time employees showed that employees within companies with recognition initiatives were four times more likely to be "extremely satisfied" with their company than employees at firms lacking recognition awards. And satisfied employees aren't likely to turn in their notice any time soon. As leaders, we can—and should—provide more positive leadership than we are doing.

So how much recognition versus criticism is enough? Tom Rath and Donald Clifton in *How Full Is Your Bucket?* suggest praise must outweigh criticism by a five-to-one margin to achieve a high-performance culture, again based on Gallup's research.

Now, some managers have been led to believe that they should maintain a balanced approach—one compliment to each criticism. But our research within dozens of the largest organizations in the world certainly confirms the five-to-one statistic, and also adds this interesting sidenote: A one-to-one ratio of positive to negative interactions is actually a harmful workplace relationship.

We are reminded of one well-meaning manager who approached us after we gave a talk at a hospital system in Texas. She said she gave her employees a handful of tokens at the beginning of the year. The employees could earn more tokens if they did great things. In December, they could trade them for an award.

"What a fun idea," we said.

"And if they make a mistake, I take a token back," she added.

"Yikes," we couldn't help saying.

Consider, for a moment, how such a one-to-one ratio would work at home with your significant other. One compliment to every criticism? How long would that work? Just think about this: How many compliments does it take at home before you are forgiven for just one criticism. "That dress is really pretty on you. You don't look so heavy."

With a one-to-one ratio with your significant other, you'd probably be sleeping on the lawn. At work, you just don't get anywhere.

Praise 'Em High

Research supporting the effectiveness of praise over criticism goes back almost a century to 1925 when Dr. Elizabeth Hurlock measured the impact of types of feedback on fourth- and sixth-grade students in a math class. In the test, one control group was praised, another was criticized, and the third was ignored. The number of math problems solved by each group was measured on days 2 through 5.

As early as day 2, students in the "praised" group were performing at a dramatically higher level than the "criticized" or "ignored" students, increasing the number of solved math problems by 71 percent during the study. In contrast, the "criticized" group increased by 19 percent and the "ignored" group by just 5 percent.

Trevor Grams, an engineer and director of operation services at EPCOR Generation Inc. in Edmonton, Alberta, Canada, explains the impact of praise versus criticism this way: "We have to be productive and get a lot done around here. And every year we have to get more done than the previous year. But that being said, we seem to get a lot more done when there is positive reinforcement than when there is negative reinforcement."

Grams, when he was still a young plant manager in Rossdale, Alberta, had an enlightening experience with a direct report—the plant's safety officer. "I had praised him right after he'd taken on some extra activities that weren't easy to be done and he'd really delivered. I entered his workspace, took the time to find him, and said thank you. He was bold enough to come to me later and talk about it. He had been thinking about it. And of the praise, he said succinctly, 'That's what it's all about.'"

In other words, the safety officer's job satisfaction wasn't based on his pay—he was well qualified and could make a similar amount elsewhere. It wasn't based on his benefits either—other firms could offer the same medical coverage. No, it was Trevor's kind of automatic feedback that helped him understand that his supervisor valued his unique strengths and contributions. And he knew he couldn't get that at another company.

People expect more heartfelt compliments than you may expect. In fact, they need at least one a week. When we tell managers that, they often guffaw and say that employees would get a big head with all those compliments.

Our friend Quint Studer, retired president of a very successful hospital and now president of the Studer Consulting Group, jokes, "Have you ever been called to your boss's office? Is your first thought: 'Well, here we go again—more reward and recognition. When are these countless compliments going to stop? They're killing my productivity.'"

Of course not. Your first thought is, "What have I done wrong now?"

Don't worry. It's very, very hard to *over* compliment your workers. No one ever checked into the Mayo Clinic with an abnormally enlarged head due to praise. It's much, much easier to come up short without recognition.

As a leader, its important to remember that specific, frequent praise isn't the warm and fuzzy side of life, it's an essential component of leadership. It's an essential in creating a great work environment.

And as the safety officer in rural Alberta knew, it was the one thing he couldn't find anywhere else.

The Tangible Rewards of Praise

Not only do employees who are praised tend to stay with their organizations—they also do their best work for them.

Consider the Watson-Wyatt Reward Plan Survey of 614 employers. It showed that the average turnover rate of employers with a clearly articulated reward strategy was 13 percent lower than that of organizations without a well-communicated plan.

And remember back to the 79 percent of employees who leave because of a lack of recognition? Compare it to recent Hewitt research that showed that in "the best" companies—where 61 percent of employees say they "trust senior management to appropriately balance employee interests with those of the organization"—79 percent of employees say they are "inspired to do their best work every day."

They say a leader is only as good as her people. With praise, you—and your employees—are always at their "best."

And as a leader, who could ask for more?

Turnover Is Costly

The thing about turnover is that it is expensive. Really expensive. More expensive than most supervisors understand.

In fact, turnover is by far the largest uncalculated expense in the corporate world.

According to William Bliss, president of Bliss & Associates, a Wayne, New Jersey, based consulting firm that provides advice for improving organizational performance, most companies take only a superficial look at turnover.

"Management assumes that it will cost maybe $5,000 to $6,000 to replace someone. But we have documented that it's actually at 150 percent of the employee's annual compensation," Bliss says, citing as an example the fact that it often costs an astonishing $75,000 to replace an employee earning $50,000.

Those are the kinds of figures that CEOs and CFOs start paying attention to.

These calculations take into account advertising costs, temporary replacement costs or overtime costs while the job is vacant, lost opportunity costs, search firm fees, relocation costs, time to interview, time to orient new hires, and time to train the new person. However, they don't and can't take into account the loss of valuable knowledge and experience, cus-

tomer service disruption, loss of client knowledge, lost sales costs, emotional costs, loss of
morale, burnout/absenteeism among remaining
employees, loss of experience, lack of continu-
ity . . . and the list goes on.

Now, here's a macro view of this problem
that we've never seen printed before: In the
United States, 4 million employees leave their
jobs every month, which is 48 million annually. With an average salary now at $34,065,
and taking a conservative cost of just 100 percent of salary to replace an employee, employee turnover costs the U.S. economy at least
$1.7 trillion annually. And that's just in the
United States. Worldwide, the number is astro-
nomical.

From a micro point of view, for those of us
managers struggling to stay ahead of competition, it's a loss that can be incalculable. Especially because the most talented employees are
often the first to leave. Why? They have the most
options and the most marketable skills.

Your best workers? It's amazing how suddenly they disappear.

Who stays with you? The nurse who can
never seem to get the IV in right, the grumbling engineer whom everyone is afraid of, the
hypochondriac maintenance worker who takes
every one of her sick days, every year. These
are the folks whose *coworkers* put their resumes on Monster.com. You think they are
ever going anywhere else? No way. You were

unfortunate enough to have hired these people in the first place, and you've got them forever.

And forever is a very, very long time.

VISIBLE TOOL

Turn Things Around

Looking for a tool to help your organization understand the cost of turnover? Here's a simple "back of the napkin" formula. Simply multiply the number of employees who willingly exit your organization (not those you terminate) by the conservative cost of 100 percent of your corporate average annual salary. For example, if you have a workforce of 500 and an average voluntary turnover rate of 15 percent, then 75 employees quit last year. If your average hourly salary is $29,700 per year, then turnover just cost you 75 times $29,700 or $2.2 million. And what would another $2.2 million mean to your bottom line?

For a more complex tool online that allows you to enter job type, benefits, and other options, go to **invisibleemployee.com** and click on Turnover.

CHAPTER THREE

The See-er

A shiver ran up Star's back. Her friend was gone and she was left behind. The Fruits of the Laborer ceremony, the noise, the singing, faded into the background. Star stretched out a hand to steady herself against a tree trunk, feeling the tingling of electricity hanging in the air where Jon had stood just moments ago. She felt dizzy...and utterly alone.

"What just happened?" she asked herself. *It couldn't be a Blink Out, right? Jon couldn't really be gone. Not Jon.*

But in her heart, she knew he was. And another question kept running through her mind: *Why now? Why didn't he stay for the Fruits of the Laborer ceremony? Wasn't that the ultimate reward?*

And then, tensing up, she realized there was another problem. She wasn't... alone. She spun and peered deeper into the dark forest—then gasped.

In the trees, not far away, a young Highlander stood, transfixed. Incredibly, he seemed to have seen Jon's sudden disappearance and was now watching her.

"Disappear!" her mind screamed. "Fade away!" But she couldn't. Or didn't want to. Some strange force was holding her there.

She saw the Highlander turn slightly and talk to the older Highlander next to him. "There's something's going on over there, in the trees," he said

The woman glanced at where he pointed, saw nothing, then scowled. "Look, I don't have time for games right now, Ian. Let's just get this stupid thing over with so we can get back to the village. I have more important things to do."

Suddenly, Star came to her senses. "What am I doing?" she cried, clenching her fists in frustration and confusion. She had been seen, the unthinkable in her tribe. She closed her eyes and concentrated on all the things the elders had said.

"You want to be safe," they had said. "You want to be comfortable. If you don't want to experience failure and criticism and exhaustion, then you must perfect the art of silence. The art of invisibility."

Star pictured the wrinkled face of the elder. In her memory, the woman's pale lips moved, "It has become our only refuge."

"It is the way," murmured Star out loud. She took a deep breath—and faded into the hillside.

∞

From his vantage point, Ian watched the shadow of the young woman move quickly away through the trees until it passed out of sight. He shook his head, wondering if he had really seen what he thought he saw, then turned back to the ceremony and tried to focus on the proceedings.

It wasn't until the moon reached its apex that the ceremonies ended. Eight of them in all—each at a different mountain.

As they made their way back to the Highlander village. Ian lagged behind the others, peering into the woods, hoping to see another Invisible Person, for now he was convinced that was what they had been.

Around him voices of Highlander's mingled with the sounds of the night.

"Some of the chests were not full this time."

"And more stones were broken."

"Paor, where's Beth? Do you have her with you?"

"Oooh, I'm going to feel this tomorrow. I'm getting too old for all this dancing around."

"Not a lot of rubies this time, and no emeralds at all. We should cut back on the offering of fruit."

But Ian barely heard. He was deep in his thoughts. Something strange was happening among the Wurc-Urs. Tomorrow night he would discuss it with the elders, during the weekly gathering. He would tell them then what he had seen in the forest. They would know what to do.

Just as Ian had thought, his news caused a strong reaction among the Highlanders. Just not the one he had expected.

"We have a word for this," said the chief elder. "Insanity."

Ian was stunned. "I'm not insane. I saw two of their people, the Invisible People. And one—a man—disappeared before my eyes. I think that's why the chests aren't as full anymore. That's why we aren't seeing the emeralds like we used to. That's why they aren't able to keep up with our demands. They're vanishing."

A few children in the group giggled and Ian turned red. The elders were frowning at him. The suspicious glances of the villagers made Ian wish *he* could fade into the shadows like the pale young woman he had seen.

"I'd like to take a trip up the mountain. I think I can find these people," he said sheepishly. "And I could talk with them. If I could understand them, learn more about them. Maybe, just maybe, we could all do better. Do more."

"You'd be wasting your time. Whoever is out there does their work without us bothering them," said an elder. "That's the way."

"They accept the half and new moon offerings," added another. "There is no need to talk to anyone. We pay them in food to deliver the jewels—it's that simple."

"And there's plenty of work to be done for you here at the village," said another.

"Crazy as a loon!" muttered a woman as she turned and left the gathering.

Ian felt his resolve weaken. Maybe they were right. They were older, more experienced. They knew the way.

Ian felt his father's arm around him. "Now, Ian, you've always been a bit of a dreamer," he warned, gently. "Forget about all this. Your job as a caretaker is to collect the jewel chests from the mountain. And you are new to it. Watch the others. Do what they do," he said as he led Ian from the great hall.

There was little to say on the way home. Both he and his father were deep in thought. Now, Ian felt more concerned about his relationship with his father than the Invisible People.

At the door to his home, he turned to his father. "I haven't shamed you, have I?"

"No," his dad shook his head and looked at the ground. "I once thought this way, too. But my father took me aside—as you will someday do with your son. It's always been done this way. And it always will. Get some sleep. Things will be clearer tomorrow."

Ian watched his father walk down the trail until he was out of sight. Then he shut the door of his cabin. Without bothering to light a candle, he fell into bed, exhausted by the emotion of the day.

But though Ian tried, he could not sleep. The reactions of the elders had come as quite a shock. All those stories told in that very hall. All the talk about the Invisible People being a *part* of the Highlanders' world. Being *important* to their success . . . even their survival.

Was it all just talk? Had he been the only one who really believed they co-existed, that there was more to this relationship than overlords and invisible servants?

In the sharp morning light, he left his house and joined the other caretakers at their observation towers. Miles away from any of the mountains, there was little to see...except that the mountain was still there. When he was young, how many years had he longed to stand here—the caretaker of a mountain—only to find there was little he could do to change what happened on the mountain? How can you make an impact on the invisible?

He shrugged. *Maybe the elders were right. Maybe I should just bear down and do my job.*

He lifted his binoculars to peer at the top of Sakas Point, *his* mountain, and imagined he could see small glints of light reflecting off the diamonds there. He couldn't help himself: In the foothills, he pictured people, real people, moving up the mountain toward them.

And then, suddenly, a question came to his mind that was so revolutionary, so frightening, that he shivered a little as he voiced it out loud.

"If *I* believe these people are important to us, then what am *I* going to do about it? Can one Highlander really make a difference?"

"You say something?" asked one of the guardians, eyeing him suspiciously.

Ian just shook his head. But somehow he couldn't shake the question. It hung there in the hot, still air, as if waiting for an answer that didn't immediately come...but was on its way.

Walking home, shoulders slouched, head down, Ian didn't look like the first See-er in hundreds of years. But already, he was.

That night he slept fitfully, dreaming of things changing: Mud huts turning into houses. Weeds blossoming into flowers. He woke, wadded up his pillow, and turned over, unaware that building inside him was the answer that would soon change everything. Not just for him, but for *everyone* on Kopani Island.

A transformation had begun.

THE SEE-ER

Modern See-ers

Today's See-ers don't see the future. They *create* the future, by *seeing people.*

The late Cotton Fitzsimmons, former coach of Phoenix Suns basketball team, had that ability. He had a genuine interest in his players—and they could sense that.

He was the kind of guy who would facilitate counseling for players with money problems or marital disputes. He gave advice when he was asked. And correction when he saw a problem—on the court or off. He was a man of principles and was an example for others. In fact, in the 1960s when racism was still a way of life in parts of the United States, he took an unpopular vocal stand and refused to eat at his favorite restaurant that had denied service to several of his African American players.

Former Phoenix Suns player Eddie Johnson recalled, "Cotton was the closest thing to a father to me as one could get. He was a guy who wasn't just a coach. He was the only coach that was really interested in your personal life."

And that ability to care for people was transforming. Not just for the individual players but for the whole Suns organization, which had certainly been struggling—finishing with just 39 wins the season before he took over. (The next year, under Fitzsimmons's direction, the same team won 48 games.)

"Players got caught up in how enthusiastic and positive he was, and he made them play better," said Jeff Hornaceck, another former player. "I'll never forget one of the first years we were in the playoffs, he and his wife JoAnn made it possible for wives to go on the trip. Little things like that are what players appreciate. I think he transformed the whole Phoenix Suns organization to the point it's at today, where players love to come to Phoenix. He was the one who changed it all from those darker times."

Fitzsimmons was so positive, that when he once took over a different team, which was in last place, he gave them a speech that centered around the word "pretend."

"You guys, when you go out there tonight, instead of remembering that we are in last place, pretend that we are in first place; instead of us being in a losing streak, pretend we are in a winning streak; instead of this being a regular game, pretend this is a playoff game."

With that, the team went on to the basketball court and were soundly beaten by the Boston Celtics. The coach was upset about the loss. But one of the players slapped him on the back and said, "Cheer up Coach! Pretend we won!"

Fitzsimmons laughed at himself. He always took his players seriously, but never himself. Just one more reason why this one man had such a remarkable impact.

Which reminds us of the Butterfly Effect, a scientific phenomenon that goes like this: A small change in the initial conditions of an experiment can drastically change long-term results. Ian Stewart, author of *Does God Play Dice? The Mathematics of Chaos*, makes this analogy: "The flapping of a single butterfly's wing today produces a tiny change in the state of the atmosphere. Over a period of time, what the atmosphere actually does diverges from what it would have done. So, in a month's time, a tornado that would have devastated the Indonesian coast doesn't happen. Or maybe one that wasn't going to happen, does."

Now picture one manager—maybe even you—making a difference. Changing your organization from darker times. Barbara Ruddy is one of the lucky employees who had one supervisor like that.

Ruddy worked at the Arizona Department of Economic Security for 30 years. Recognition was sparse over the first decade and a half. In fact, her 5- and 10-year service awards arrived impersonally in the mail. Her 15-year award arrived an amazing three years late, because her boss couldn't be bothered to fill in the paperwork.

But her 20-year service award was different. Her new boss gathered colleagues. He delved into her personnel file and regaled the group by listing every job Ruddy had held in the department for the past two decades. "Near the end," said Ruddy, "he thanked me for all I had brought to the department. I had tears in my eyes. No one had ever recognized me in front of my peers before."

Ruddy was so moved by this simple presentation, she asked to take over the department's recognition program, so she could teach managers how to make effective service award presentations that would have an emotional impact on employees and bond them to their organization.

In just a few minutes, Ruddy's boss transformed her work experience. And, in turn, she transformed an entire organization's culture. The great thing is, Ruddy's story doesn't have to be all that unique. All managers have the potential for that kind of influence . . . if they choose to tap it.

The trouble is, most managers think they are doing just fine in this regard. One CEO told us as we began this work that we were starting in a hole. "You've got to understand," he said, "everyone thinks they're a nice guy."

But in reality, genuinely nice bosses are hard to find. And when we find one, we stay and we stay committed.

It Had to Be You

You might not realize how much influence you actually have on your employees. Here's a great fact: Did you know that to employees, your opinion matters more than the CEO's? *Incentive Magazine* reports that when asked from whom they would rather receive praise, 57 percent of respondents chose their direct supervisor, while only 21 percent would rather be praised by the company president.

Survey after survey shows that employees most value the opinions of their direct supervisors. They want to get information from them. They take their cues for attitude, commitment, and loyalty from them. And the real impact of any message happens at the managerial or supervisory level.

When bosses recognize and value employees, things change for the better. When they don't, things change . . . but in a different way.

It's called turnover.

Talk about a perfect example, just a few months ago, we talked to Rob, a programmer at a small, struggling company in the insurance industry. He told us that despite the opportunity for greater pay elsewhere, he's stayed at this troubled company for five years. Why? "Because I like my supervisor and the atmosphere here is so great."

Interestingly enough, Rob contacted us again recently to say that he was putting out resumes. When we asked him what had changed, he gave us just two words: "My supervisor."

For Rob, getting a new boss changed the entire working atmosphere. And it happens more often than you think.

Showing Your Love

An old Saturday-morning cartoon featured twins—a brother and a sister—called the Wonder Twins. Maybe you remember them. By touching their magic rings together, they could transform into anything they wanted.

"Wonder Twin powers activated! Form of a snake!" they would shout. And then they would go out and save the world.

Managers have a similar transforming power. But unfortunately, too many are pointed in the wrong direction. They are so focused on gaining their immediate manager's or senior management's approval, that they forget to listen, to see, and recognize the people in their charge. They aren't *in touch* with their employees. And in these environments, nothing great ever happens.

What is amazing is that in the majority of work cultures, senior leaders actually consciously or unconsciously encourage this behavior. In the most toxic of these cultures, an older manager will take aside a new supervisor to explain "the way": that employees are typically lazy and devious, that they must be dealt with harshly, and that recognition comes every two weeks in a paycheck.

But in the most common cultures, these supervisory lessons are much more subtle. By giving managers no approved tools to recognize their people and no guidelines on appropriate rewards for above-and-beyond behavior, line leaders either do nothing or are forced to hide the evidence of their employee appreciation from leadership.

A year ago, we conducted focus group sessions with four sets of line managers and then with four groups of human resources (HR) professionals in San Francisco, New York, and

Atlanta. We wanted to gauge each group's informal recognition activities.

What we found was revealing. The groups of HR folks, who represent the formal people policies of senior leadership in the firms, said their managers had very little budget for informal or day-to-day recognition. When asked if they thought managers were spending money on recognition anyway, several HR staff members responded with indignation. Said one, "Our managers wouldn't break corporate rules."

And yet, most of the people in the manager groups said they *were* recognizing their employees. They had to, they said, if they wanted to maintain morale and achieve their goals. But, just about everyone admitted the recognition wasn't really in line with the company's policies, and most thought they'd get in trouble if senior management found out about their spending.

Here are a few examples:

"I just took my team go-carting," said a fellow in Atlanta. "I don't know if that met corporate policy . . . if it was appropriate or not."

"At least once a month I'll take one or two of my people to lunch at Chili's or a steak house as a reward," said another manager in New York.

A woman in the same group sheepishly admitted, "Oh yeah, I took my team and their spouses out to dinner to celebrate two weeks ago. I coded the receipt to my supplies budget. I don't know if I'm going to get fired about it, but I don't care."

We think she actually does care, or she wouldn't have been so nervous about admitting it . . . and wouldn't have had to scrimp on copier toner the rest of the month.

SET: Managers First and Foremost Set the Vision

To most employees, mission statements and strategy maps are full of high-level gobbledygook that doesn't mean a thing. Great leaders translate those pretty words into daily activities. They *SET* clear team priorities, based on company or area goals. In other words, they help employees understand what matters most around here.

Once workers have a clear and understandable goal to focus on, they typically can accomplish it. Because, when it comes right down to it, most workers want to do a good job. They want to make management happy. They just need to know how.

In fact, when asked to define what sets their jobs apart, employees with the most satisfying, profitable, and productive work experiences reply that they know what is expected of them.

In the best-case scenarios, management at the very top level of an organization understands the need for clear and concise goals and creates language to reflect it.

Take for example Friendly's Ice Cream. With $600 million in revenue annually from more than 500 restaurants in the eastern United States, as well as ice cream distribution efforts, the company is robust and well managed. They have a clear corporate vision: "To be the leading casual full service restaurant/ice cream shoppe and premium retail ice cream brand in the eastern United States . . . known for operations excellence, great signature foods, famous ice cream shoppe desserts, sparkling clean facilities, prompt, friendly service and dedicated, talented people . . . resulting in outstanding customer loyalty and consistent profitable growth."

But all those great words are just that, words, without clear direction from line managers. Friendly's vision is translated into action in manager Beverly Gomez's restaurant in Hershey, Pennsylvania. "When I hire people, I map out my specific expectations and accountabilities for them—the ground rules if you will," said Gomez. "If you stay, you are going to have to do this and this. I do, everyone does. I mop floors. I clean toilets. The whole team follows the rules and works like a team. You've got to be very clear with the rules, responsibilities, and accountabilities up front. And I stress respect from the first interview. I expect them to respect each other, and in turn I give respect." But, she added, "I don't expect them to respect me, I'll earn that."

Gomez follows up by recognizing the right behaviors in all her 77 employees. "Recognition is a great communicator," she said. "It shows employees what their peers are doing and how they are doing it, even how the business is going. By recognizing people, they see the business is doing okay. And best of all, it helps set the standards of what my expectations are."

And, of course, it spells out what that lofty vision really means in Hershey.

In your firm, it's your job to provide the translation, taking "We work strategically with our customers to improve their performance," all the way down to "Our washers are accurate to within 1/100th of a millimeter." And "We are the leader in customer response and care," to "We pride ourselves on answering calls within 30 seconds and resolving 95 percent of client issues on the first call."

At EPCOR Generation in Edmonton, Alberta, Canada, Trevor Grams, director of operation services, says the process of *SET* begins high above him with a strategy map created by upper management. "From there, we create our division strategy map and that provides more clarity to individual directors and managers and our groups. . . . That becomes the template to develop each person's performance management tool."

Goals are set for each individual that align with business unit and corporate goals. Then, and this is key, leaders list the *behaviors that support these goals.* The specific behaviors that employees should focus on.

"A good practice is to identify just four or five things, so people can focus and make a noticeable improvement in those areas," said Grams.

Grams has seen dramatic changes as a result of clarifying goals. One employee in his
training area was given the goal to learn how
his role affects the rest of the company so he
could make better decisions and best deliver
training services that would impact the entire
organization. After 20 years at one facility,
Grams noted that this employee had lost a big-
picture perspective.

The goal was clear. But Grams went one step
further than most managers would. He defined
the desired *behaviors* that would help the employee achieve his goal. For example, one expected behavior was "Interact at least weekly
with key decision makers in other areas of
the company." Given the opportunity—and encouragement—to branch out, the employee
blossomed.

"As soon as he started developing key rela-
tionships with key individuals in other business
areas, his perspective and his training offerings
began to change. He was expressing things from
a corporate-needs perspective," said Grams.

All that improvement from just three letters:
S, E, and T.

SET the Right Goals

The important thing is to make sure you get the
translation right. A few years ago, a friend of
ours was traveling by commercial jet out of the
Pittsburgh airport.

The flight had left the gate and was en route to the runway when the pilot announced a dreaded ground stop due to inclement weather. After the first two hours stuck in a tight coach seat on the crowded, grounded plane, our friend pressed the call button and asked for the flight attendant.

He believed he spoke for everyone when he said, "We want to go back to the gate."

The attendant explained that they would then lose their place in line for takeoff and the ground stop might be lifted within just a few minutes.

It was another three hours before the plane made its way back to the gate and our friend— a giant of a guy who played college football at the University of Pittsburgh—was allowed out of his tiny seat.

After this horrific experience, he did a little digging and discovered the real reason planes at this airline were remaining on the tarmac: Airline quality at this time was scored by the number of on-time departures, which was measured by when they left the gate, not by when the plane actually left the ground. The airline had decided on-time delivery was their number one priority. And, in turn, had sacrificed customer satisfaction for the statistic.

It was an airline with a one-way ticket to nowhere.

A company without defined goals—or, worse yet—*mis*defined goals will never succeed at getting the best from their employees. On the other hand, leaders at all levels who communicate clear, strategic goals can take their organizations anywhere.

For them, the sky's the limit.

SEE: Great Managers Are Observant

Paul Smucker, Former J. M. Smucker and Company CEO, once said, "Listen with your full attention, look for the good in others, have a sense of humor, and say thank you for a job well done."

That's just what we were going to say! Smucker was right. In this world, there are many managers who are smart and competent, who have background and credentials. But there is a dearth of great managers who take the time to listen to their employees and actively look for achievements.

One of our favorite leaders is Quint Studer. In 1996, Studer moved to Florida to become administrator of the 492-bed Baptist Hospital. When this innovative leader started at the facility, he didn't park next to the front door in the administrator's reserved spot, but in the farthest lot. And he talked to employees on the long walk. He also daily made the rounds of the facility, talking to employees, and saying, "Hi, my name is Quint Studer. I'm the new administrator here. I work for you. What should I do today?"

Says Studer, from the way they looked at him, he suspected many were going to suggest, "Take a urine screen."

But pretty quickly, very simple ideas started to flow. A nurse said, "Tonight, when I leave, it's going to be dark. We work in a pretty tough neighborhood. I park out by the bushes and they haven't been trimmed in months. I'm worried when I go out to my car that someone could be hiding there. Could you get those bushes trimmed?"

During the next 12 hours, while she was working, Studer had the bushes clipped and he even had maintenance put up a small fence. When the nurse went out to her car, she noticed that Studer had listened. She felt safe and knew that leadership cared about her as an individual.

In his years there, by focusing on employee satisfaction, something remarkable happened. Patient satisfaction—which had ranged between the 9th and 40th percentiles—soared to the 99th percentile of hospitals nationally. Turnover dropped by 18 percent, and the organization's financials were rock solid. Moody's even upgraded the bond rating of the hospital, and Baptist is consistently ranked in the top 100 best places to work by *Fortune* magazine.

What leaders like Studer learn about their employees (their fears, strengths, weaknesses, wants, and needs) gives these managers the ability to motivate effectively and strategically channel employee efforts. That's why it's usually true that behind every great employee, you'll find an exceptional boss.

Doug Shannon, of T. Rowe Price's Client Operations, is one example. Recently, he volunteered for double duty while his manager was on an extended five-month maternity leave—doing many of her duties in addition to his own. He felt safe doing so, because he knew his efforts would be appreciated.

He was right. In return, for his exceptional contributions, Shannon received his company's Extraordinary Achievement Award in a public recognition ceremony. It's part of an overall employee recognition program that has also significantly improved client satisfaction scores.

When we met Shannon we asked him about his contribution. A self-deprecating fellow, he shrugged and said, "They are really good around here about recognizing you when you go above and beyond." Being wise guys, we then asked what if T. Rowe Price was not good at recognizing, would he have made the same contribution?

Shannon politely shrugged and asked for the next question.

In the Detroit area, Cynthia Parrish, a Mount Clemens General Hospital nurse assistant, received her organization's Strength of Purpose Award for superior patient care that demonstrates compassion—one of the hospital's core values. Since the program was initiated, employee turnover has been cut in half and the bed vacancy rate is among the lowest in the region.

Sure, hospitals demand a lot from their employees. In this high-pressure environment, mistakes can cost more than money or lost opportunities, they can take a life. But remember back to the school students in 1925, where one group was praised, one was criticized, and one was ignored. No matter where you work—in health care, in union environments, on a nuclear sub in the Pacific, even in the most intense of workplaces—when employee efforts are noticed and recognized by their supervisors, employees are more likely to make the right decisions.

Get Out of the Office

An important step toward recognition is to step out of your office every day and talk to your employees.

An advertisement for SteelCase office furniture reads, "Interoffice mail. E-mail. Voice Mail. Whatever happened to Face-Mail?"

Good question. It's one a lot of employees are asking.

This may be embarrassingly simple, but when we ask employees and employee groups about their supervisors and managers, the first complaint is typically that they don't even say hello every day. And while it does sound elementary, greeting and meeting is actually an essential part of creating an engaged workforce. And it is impossible to do that from your office. It's a little-known fact that most supervisors are a little far-sighted. And no wonder; it's hard to focus on your people from the boardroom or your new corner office. It's easier to see employee challenges and interests and successes when you are up close.

Intel Chairman Gordon Moore has taken his own approach to face time. In fact, he has taken it to new levels. He, and everyone else in the company, work in open cubicles. Even more unusual, whenever the chairman is in his cubicle, the door is open to employees. If there *was* a door, that is.

No corner office. No intimidating leather furniture. No hurdles to communication. No kidding.

Looks like, for leadership, the times are a-changin'.

And most of us recognize that. These days when we meet with supervisors and tell them they must be seen more, most readily agree that this should be a priority. Once, however, an entrenched leader said, "If I just start showing up all of a sudden, my employees will be suspicious."

It reminded us of a manager who tried this and got it all wrong. He spent more time with his group, but just ended up criticizing more and directing nitty-gritty details. Behind his back, his employees began complaining about his new ability to drop in just long enough to dump on everyone and then leave. They began calling him the Seagull.

We recommend getting out of the office for a solid block of time—30 minutes or more—at least once a day. While there, concentrate on asking questions and listening, not dumping. As leaders, we spend an inordinate amount of time giving orders and not nearly enough time listening.

Besides showing interest in their specific work projects—short term and long—make it a point to ask employees about their hobbies, families, or other interests outside the job. Ask about the model of the 1968 Mustang on their top shelf, the family members in the photo taped to their computer, the print of the Monet painting on the wall, or why they'd choose a picture of karate legend Bruce Lee to grace their desk. Ask where they like to go to lunch. Find out where their best vacation was and where they plan to go this year.

Knowing your employee's favorite candy bar or that he is afraid of heights will prove invaluable when the time comes to recognize him. (You'll probably want to pass on a hot-air balloon ride as a reward.)

As you listen to your employees take notes on what you find—personal and professional. You think you'll remember, but trust us, you'll soon forget. To keep track, some managers tell us that they carry around a small notepad or make notes in their handheld computer. Others reserve a block of time to type information into the computer or on a notebook immediately following their daily visit.

It may sound trivial, but this one little step will succeed in setting you apart as a leader. Although few leaders really listen, even fewer follow up on what they hear. Thoreau may have been speaking for all employees when he said, "The greatest compliment anyone gave me was when they asked me for my opinion and then attended to my answer."

Now, in the interest of total disclosure, we should warn you: The process of getting to know and recognize your employees will be awkward at first. You may get it wrong a few times. But keep trying. The same is true of learning to walk or ski or even learning to drive. But you did it. And you got better with practice. And imagine if you hadn't taken the leap. It's hard to get respect professionally when your teenage son has to drop you off and pick you up from work.

Remember: No pain, no gain. And trust us, it's worth the pain. Setting clear goals and seeing employee successes paves the way for the next step in creating a place where people want to work. And that is *Celebrating.*

And who doesn't like a party?

BREAKING THE BREAD BARRIER

They say money can't buy happiness. But we've never seen a sad person piloting a 60-foot luxury yacht. They look pretty happy to us.

Still, as an employee motivator, money has been proven to have little staying power. And yet, for as long as companies have offered incentives to make people work harder, employees have requested money over any other reward. And managers give in.

"I'd rather have the cash," says your employee.

"But we are giving out $7 movie tickets."

"I don't care, I want the cash."

For once, we'd recommend not listening to your employees.

Why? For starters, cash as a reward—unless we are talking thousands of dollars—is much less memorable than rewards of merchandise, travel, and other tangible objects. In a Wirthlin Worldwide survey of 1,010 award recipients, 29 percent of those who received cash bonuses paid bills with the money. Another 18 percent could not remember where the money went. While 11 percent bought household items. Nothing memorable about paying the gas bill, now is there?

Another serious problem for leaders is the entitlement that cash creates. It very quickly becomes part of an employee's salary. Give someone a $200 cash bonus one year, and what do they expect the next? At least the same amount.

Next, tangible rewards have trophy value that have an increased perception in employees' minds. Here's a simple case in point. Say it's the holidays and you have $25 per person to spend on a gift. It's quite easy to add that amount to their paycheck. And they end up with about $15 after taxes. How many thanks would you get on January 1? Zip. How many employees would think, "I busted my butt for him all year. I guess it was worth fifteen bucks?" Probably everyone.

Now, instead, let's say you use that meager amount to order a few $25 gift baskets and have them sent to each employee's home—filled with a few festive foods. And say you include a handwritten note of specific thanks from you to each employee. How many employees would remember your thoughtfulness? Just about everyone.

So instead of cash, focus your rewards on tangible items that can be used over and over again, can be displayed or worn, or can be enjoyed with family or friends. A great award evokes memories of how it was earned, who gave it, and what business goal was met.

And unlike cash, that knowledge never goes away.

VISIBLE TOOL

Welcoming New Employees and Reconnecting with Everyone

We are often asked for the secret to motivation. And we answer (only slightly tongue-in-cheek): First, try not to kill it.

Most employees, after all, begin a job with a desire to succeed and achieve. Just consider the jobs you have arrived at. Have you ever begun a new position with a sense of dread—quickly trying to find ways to cut corners or shirk your responsibility? Of course not. Almost everyone who starts a job is pumped, hoping this will be the company to (finally) meet their needs.

But the first 90 days are critical. If the job doesn't meet an employee's personal needs in the first three months, morale declines sharply. And from there, employee motivation is often doomed to suffer a slow and painful death, as well.

But it doesn't have to be that way. Great managers know that it's much easier to keep motivation alive and build on it than to let it die and then try to revive it. So they determine early in employment what motivates each individual—and provide the type of recognition people crave.

And we've found that one of the most effective ways to find out what motivates an employee is to ask. (Revolutionary as that may sound.) We recommend meeting privately with new employees during their first days at the office to do just that. Don't combine the meeting with anything else. Don't go over your expectations at this point. Don't have them sign any health care papers.

You may wish to begin the interview by saying something like, "Since you are going to be a vital part of our team, I want to be able to express my appreciation for your extra efforts. Some employees like to be recognized in public, while others prefer quiet, personal recognition. When it's your time to be recognized, I want to provide it in the style you like best."

Then ask:

1. What type of celebration do you prefer?
   - Private: A sincere thank you without a lot of attention from coworkers, maybe over a lunch.
   - Informal: Recognition from my manager at a staff meeting in front of peers.
   - Formal: An award celebration with coworkers and guests.
2. What recognition gifts do you like?
   - Dinner for two
   - Attending a training class or seminar

- Spa gift certificate
- Music CDs or tapes
- Book by favorite author
- Tickets to a ball game
- Tickets to the theatre, ballet, symphony
- Opportunity to work on a high-profile project
- Time off
- Other: _____

3. Who would you prefer present an award to you?
   - Your manager
   - The person who nominated you for the award
   - Senior management

4. What type of day-to-day recognition would you appreciate?
   - Handwritten thank you note/card
   - Typed letter for your personnel file
   - Certificate of achievement
   - Engraved trophy or other memento

5. Can we publicize your achievements in the company newsletter?

6. If you had a day to spend as you choose, describe what you would do and where you would go.

Of course, this is just the beginning. Getting to know employees requires consistent, daily interaction. But this simple interview gives you a head start. The interview itself is a form of recognition of an employee's potential. And the knowledge you glean will allow you to follow up with appropriate recognition during the very first week of employment.

By the way, this type of interview also is a good way to begin rebuilding a relationship with an employee whose motivation level is flagging.

So, remember, when in doubt . . . go ahead and *ask.*

For other great ideas on how to engage your employees, sign up for our monthly Carrot Culture newsletter online at **invisibleemployee.com**.

CHAPTER FOUR

Recognizing

Ian was working his plan. It had taken him a while to think of it—and even more time to find the nerve to try it. Now, in the predawn light, he heaved the basket of fruit and grain down heavily at the offering spot. It landed with a loud thump. Ian rubbed his shoulder. It was his second trip to the mountain with a bonus offering in as many weeks.

He had thought extra fruit and greens would be just what the workers needed, but the results had been disappointing. Each day the basket was empty, so the offering had been accepted. But there was no sign of improvement in the quantity of jewels.

He knelt and fingered the cracked gems in the bottom of a chest. No change in the quality either. He started to close the chest...but thought better of it. He had an idea.

Why not? he reasoned, as he dug into his pocket, finding a small piece of parchment. Carefully, he wrote in his best script:

"Thank you for your good work. Great job."

He rocked back on his heels and considered the insincere words for a moment, then crumpled the paper up. He took out another piece and tried again:

"I noticed 40 undamaged gems were added to the chest today and they look incredible! I know it takes a lot of effort to treat them gently and protect them from damage. So thank you for those efforts."

He centered the paper on top of the gems and shut the chest.

Now, he could only wait and see.

It was another week before he could return to the offering spot. And it surprised him how nervous he felt as he opened the chest.

The note was gone and in its place was a pile of gems. Yes, some were still broken, but most were intact. It was an improvement, he thought with a smile. Two other chests were full too, with equally high-quality gems. He glanced around the clearing. Were the Invisible People there now, watching him, unseen?

This time he wrote:

"This week's harvest is vastly improved. There are fewer broken stones than I have seen in many years. Your efforts have not gone unnoticed. Thank you so much for your care!"

He could hardly keep himself from jumping for joy as he walked down the mountain. Only the thought that he might be watched helped him maintain his dignity until he had bolted the door of his house.

It had worked! He allowed himself a few moments of jubilation then settled down to the bigger question—What to do next. The answer now was plain to see.

∞

While it might be easy to see what needed to be done, the problem was doing it. That became clear just an hour after starting up the mountain. Although Ian had left before dawn, sweat dripped off his forehead and into his eyes. He was running out of breath, too, since the air was thinner at this altitude.

"Admit it, Ian, you're just out of shape," he said to himself. "And way out of your comfort zone."

He had not expected the mountain trail to be this difficult. He had even brought a bag to gather jewels along the way. But he had seen none. Probably he hadn't made it high enough. Or maybe they were harder to find than he thought. Oh, well. Even if he did spot some, he wondered if he'd have the strength to carry a heavy rucksack down.

He'd planned to go higher, but at a large boulder his legs gave out. So Ian left the trail and sat down behind it . . . to wait and watch in the shade.

It wasn't long before he heard footsteps along the trail—coming down. It was the same woman he had seen before in the clearing when the tall man had disappeared, but this time she was carrying bags bulging with jewels.

Ian smiled. But when he looked at the woman's face, he saw only anger and frustration. She was muttering to herself as she set the sacks down on top of the boulder.

"Congratulations, Star. You got another full bag of stones. I don't know why I even try. What's the point? I can't do it all alone."

She kicked a stone lying on the ground.

Suddenly, Ian felt the hairs on his neck rise. There was a strange electricity in the air. The woman straightened and rubbed her arms. Ian noticed the woman's pale, translucent skin, and realized that she seemed to fade in and out of focus. In a flash, he remembered the young man with the blond hair and the sudden disappearance in the woods. Was she about to Blink Out?

"Wait!" Ian yelled. And without thinking, he stepped out into the open.

The woman froze, facing him in disbelief. But she did not disappear.

Ian froze, too. And found, to his horror, that he had no idea what to say.

"You can see me?" the woman cried out.

Ian understood her words, although they were laced with a thick accent.

"I came to thank you for the gems," Ian's voice caught in his throat. The woman stared at him uncomprehendingly. Maybe she didn't understand him. "I, I left you the notes... in the chest."

A grudging sign of acknowledgment crossed the woman's face.

"You—" Ian was about to continue when a high panicked voice rang from below in the foothills.

"Star! Come quick! It's Lee!"

Without a word, the woman raced down the path, raising a cloud of dust and leaving the bags of gems behind. Ian stood there for a moment more, then picked the bags up and followed as quickly as he could.

But she was too fast. And although he waited for hours, he didn't see her again that day.

That night as he sat and stared out the window at the falling rain, he wondered if he had really stopped the woman from vanishing by appearing at the right moment. It had seemed that way. Had he changed things just by *seeing* her? An idea was taking shape in his mind. A crazy idea. But...he couldn't help but wonder....

"Can I stop the disappearances simply by recognizing the Wurc-Urs?" he asked aloud.

It was improbable, impossible, absolutely insane...but he knew he had to find out.

A few days passed before Ian found himself sitting behind the boulder on the mountain again. He had been there two hours, and was about to start back down the path, when he heard footsteps coming up the trail. It was the same woman. They had called her Star. So she hadn't given up after all! Ian smiled. Yet, something about her was different. She was more visible than the first night he had seen her. He was sure of it! Not translucent, and yet not solid yet, either. He noticed she had someone with her.

"Um, nice morning," Ian said as he stepped onto the trail. It was the first formal greeting from a Highlander to a group of Wurc-Urs in generations, and he had spit out, "Um, nice morning." He wanted to whack his forehead in disgust.

Star nodded back. Ian noticed that although she was wary, she wasn't startled. She must have been expecting me, Ian thought. Star reached back to gently pull a very young woman from behind her. The girl was small, but with a strong, muscular build and translucent skin. Ian thought he might be able to see right through her if he looked closely enough. *She's like a ghost,* he thought, and he wondered if she were in the last stages before disappearing.

"Lee, this is the man I told you about, the See-er."

The See-er? Ian realized with surprise that he had not told her his name.

"This is my sister, Lee," continued Star, in her thick accent. "I wanted you to see her. You can see her, can't you?"

Ian nodded. "Yes. I can see her. She travels quickly, like you."

Star smiled. "Yes, she does. I'm so glad you can see her."

∞

Star didn't know why she was so happy, but something positive was happening for her sister. She had been so worried about Lee since the day they had found her quickly fading from view.

"Do you climb the mountain every day?" asked Ian.

"Yes. Several times a day. There are so few of us, now. Especially up high."

Star and Lee led Ian slowly up the trail, taking a slower pace on his account. She explained which gems were found at different elevations. She even helped Ian find his first common sapphire to add to the bag. Eventually, Star explained in passionate detail the threat created by the Blink Outs. Then, turning a corner, she paused at a sharp drop off that fell to the foothills below.

"And this is a spot where we used to drop the bags filled with gems," she said, smiling ruefully. "But not so much anymore."

Ian said little, just listened and watched. And yet, as the hours passed, he realized he was learning more than any Highlander ever had about the mountains and the people who climbed them in search of gems.

In no time, it seemed, the sun was low on the horizon and they were heading down the mountain with bags full of precious stones. Ian noticed with pleasure that little Lee looked less translucent—the palest shade of pink.

It's working, he thought, as he walked home through the woods in twilight. What could be better than this?

It didn't take long to find out. The next day, as Ian reached the boulder, he was met with a surprise. Six pale Wurc-Urs were already there, waiting...no, *wanting* to be seen.

It had been weeks since Ian had been to his observation tower. He had been spending more time on the mountain and his face was tanned and the blisters on his feet were almost all healed. He wanted to share what was happening on his mountain with the other caretakers. Maybe it would help them, too.

When he reached the platform, the other Highlanders eyed him without warmth.

"Look who it is," said one. "It's the king of the mountain."

Several caretakers laughed.

"You've been up there an awful lot," said another. "Are you gathering the jewels yourself?"

Ian opened his mouth to reply, but was cut off.

"Nothing good will come of it," said another, looking ominous.

After a moment, Ian shook his head and picked up his rucksack to leave.

∞

But good things are happening, thought Ian as he walked toward the mountain. No one was tossing the bags down his mountain anymore, so there were fewer broken jewels in his chests. That had been his first priority. And some Wurc-Urs had begun climbing higher, in search of emeralds, although no one had brought one down yet.

"Ian!" The voice sounded distant.

He looked up the trail. Far off, he could see someone waving at him with both arms. The person began to move down the trail quickly, kicking up a cloud of dust and yelling something Ian couldn't quite catch.

Was someone hurt? Ian began to sprint toward the person.

It was Star. Ian could hear her before he could see her.

"I did it! I got them!" she yelled. Ian slumped a little with relief. It was triumph, not panic, in her voice.

"I got the first emerald! I did it!" yelled Star, holding up a bag. "I know where they are. And I can show the others!" she said, thrusting the bag toward Ian. "Look!"

Opening the bag, Ian found it filled with sea green stones—more than he had seen in a lifetime.

"I knew it would be you," said Ian. "Star, no one has brought down an emerald for a long time. This requires a celebration."

All the way down the mountain, Star told Ian about her journey. How she had gotten up early. How she had almost given up, but had decided to go a little farther. How she had found an unexplored crevasse. Ian listened with delight to the details.

At the bottom of the hill, Star left to tell her family, and Ian recruited help from the Wurc-Urs in preparing a special feast. He then went to a secluded spot to think of the appropriate words to share. He thought of how Star still idolized Jon, the man who he had seen blink out. She talked of him often. And, he remembered her bringing her little sister, Lee, to the mountain to be "seen." And what she had said just now, "I can show the others," well, maybe that meant she craved a little more responsibility.

That evening, when all the Wurc-Urs were off the mountain, they gathered around the campfire. Word had spread about Star's accomplishment and their eyes shone expectantly. There had been several celebrations in recent weeks—and they had come to look forward to them, Ian knew.

He stood and said, "As you know, today we made history."

He held aloft the bag filled with the green jewels. The Wurc-Urs whooped and yelled.

"One of us did something that has not been done in many years. Star, would you come over here?"

Blushing, Star joined him by the firelight.

"Today, Star brought down the first bag of emeralds I have ever seen!"

He poured them out gently onto the ground, where they sparkled like tiny green fires. The Wurc-Urs erupted into cheers.

Ian waited for the noise to die down, then said. "Star climbed with Jon before he Blinked Out. He could see her potential. You'll remember that Jon was one of the first, long ago, to bring down a diamond. And I think he would be proud of her today."

Star dipped her head and Ian could see her blinking furiously.

"Star knows the way to the emerald fields. You all know she is a quick, skilled climber. She is careful and safe. She will now be leading a group of Wurc-Urs to the emerald field each day. And I would like Lee to be the first member of her team."

He took one large, star-shaped emerald and strung it quickly onto a strand of leather rope. The necklace he then placed around Star's neck. "This is to remember forever, Star, the day you brought the first emerald off Sakas Mountain."

Amid the cheers, spontaneous dancing broke out. Music started to play. And Star began to cry.

RECOGNIZING

Celebrate

It's an easy solution to throw money at our employee problems—as if higher salaries will enhance productivity or generate ideas or cultivate customer intimacy. While competitive salaries are important, going above market won't drive greater performance. In reality, real solutions are much less expensive: Each of your employees wants to be seen, to be validated and recognized.

"Recognition is America's most underused motivational tool," says Richard Kovacevich, Chairman and CEO of Wells Fargo. Kovacevich is one executive who has discovered that in a recognition culture, it's impossible for employees to be invisible for long.

In this section, we'll discuss the elements of effective praise and recognition: specific, sincere, public, appropriate—and frequent.

Be Specific

General praise has no impact.

Let us say that again: General praise has no impact on people.

If you've ever watched a great Little League coach in action, you may have wondered how he or she gets so much out of a team. What's the secret—other than the ability to be heard over 10 screaming kids? The difference between great kids' coaches and lousy ones is not just their knowledge of game, but how they interact with their players.

You've probably seen the kind of coach who screams at everything—imagining he's Bill Parcells on the sidelines. The result is a field of terrified tots, kids who live in constant fear of making a mistake and provoking the coach's wrath. As a result, they play it safe. The team might be pretty good with this leadership, but it will never be great.

And chances are, most of the kids won't play again next year.

Then, there's the coach who thinks he's Mr. Rogers. He doesn't keep score. He doesn't keep stats. He pats everyone on the back as they leave the field, saying, "Great job, great job, great job." Everyone is just fantastic. He's motivating the masses.

Well, actually he's not. But he thinks he is.

Then, in a few rare cases, there are coaches who use specific, timely praise to teach the principles of the game: "Tony, you got down in front of that grounder like I told you. You didn't get it this time, but you got a nice bruise! Great effort." Or, "Brinden, you really stretched for that ball on first. That gave you an extra foot and what happened? Right, you got the guy out. Doesn't that feel great?"

Much better than the ubiquitous "great job," don't you think? Trust us, the kids do.

And so do employees.

Whatever you do to recognize employees, please, please don't turn into the manager who strides through the factory with finger guns blazing, firing out glib, "Great job you," or "Hey, keep up the good work." That kind of general praise motivates no one. In fact, it feels a little demeaning and makes employees wonder, "Does that bozo even know what I do around here?"

But when a supervisor can stand up and brag about your specific achievements for 10 minutes, it's impossible to think she doesn't know what's going on around the office. It's also impossible to feel invisible. In fact, it's darn near impossible to feel anything less than 10 feet tall.

Here's a great example of specific praise at the workplace, given during a recent performance award presentation we attended at the $3 billion insurance firm Westfield Group in Ohio. The leader, Bob, is presenting an award to Brian in front of his peers.

BOB: It's my honor to give Brian a platinum award, the highest award we can give in Westfield Excellence. This is a big deal. How many platinum awards have we given out this year?

GROUP MEMBER: Six.

BOB: Wow. Six. Don't let this go to your head, Brian. [Everyone laughs. Bob grabs Brian by the shoulder. Brian looks at Bob with genuine warmth.]

BOB: This award is for something Brian did on his own time. We were going down to a conference in Florida and wanted to demonstrate our WestComm product. What Brian did was go out on his own, get the type of software that would help us demonstrate this system. He learned it on his own, put it all together on his own. It made a huge difference in our ability to showcase that product. And it's so good that we are taking it to our marketing folks and we are taking it outside. [Cheers]

BRIAN: Wow [with an aw-shucks grin and a nod].

BOB: Brian, you really do epitomize what we are all about at Westfield. You demonstrated our core capability of Self-Development, which helped enhance our Customer Focus— our most important goal. So thanks and congratulations.

Brief, Sure. But a great recognition moment? You bet. And we're sure Brian felt the same way.

The difference between a great moment and a lousy one is being specific to what matters most in your team or company. And to be specific, you have to be prepared. In the previous chapter, we encouraged you to keep a record of interesting facts you learn about employees. (See page 65.) Doing this will give you information to work with during your presentation.

Here's how to use it: In advance of the presentation, schedule a brief block of uninterrupted time to prepare what you are going to say. Take out your log of the employee action and review it. Make some notes. This process doesn't have to take an hour, it can be 5 or 10 minutes if you are fast. Just enough time to consider what specific accomplishments you'll talk about, whether you would like to involve anyone else in the presentation—a current coworker or someone from another department, and to double-check any information about the employee you may be unsure of.

The few minutes of time you spend in advance will pay off in the recognition moment when the employee feels truly appreciated.

Sincerity Counts!

It's hard to be sincere without preparation. Because, while you might be able to bluff through a staff meeting, it's almost impossible to bluff a recognition moment.

There is nothing worse than a poorly prepared supervisor who actually gets the award recipient's name wrong (we've heard this story at least two dozen times). Or gets the facts messed up. Or can't think of much to say. But wait. On second thought, maybe there is something worse. The prize for worst recognition moment has to be the one where the executives simply didn't bother to attend.

First, a great dinner in a very good restaurant is often a nice way to recognize your top people. It gets employees out of the office and lets them experience the luxury of a fine meal that they wouldn't normally lavish on themselves. Even better is when the dinner is with a top executive in your organization. It shows that upper management cares, and employees get a chance to express their ideas and successes with a person who can make things happen.

A long-time friend of ours works in Manhattan's financial district and is one of the best portfolio managers in his firm. He has been a top performer for many years. Recently, his company decided to honor the top seven managers with dinner at a very expensive restaurant in the city. All seven received a beautiful invitation to meet at the restaurant at a certain time on a specific evening.

The day arrived and our friend worked late, as usual, and then headed over to the restaurant. It would be a nice evening to rub shoulders with the top dogs in the company. He was genuinely excited.

When he arrived at the restaurant, he didn't see anyone he knew. Not his boss or his boss's boss. He waited a while, hemmed and hawed, and then he noticed that there were a few other people doing the same thing. Almost simultaneously, they came together and asked each other where they worked. You guessed it! They were the top seven. They went to the reservation manager and discovered that there was indeed a reservation. But for just the seven of them: no bosses. Just seven employees who had never met before having dinner together. No rubbing of shoulders. No award presentation.

Of course, they ordered the most expensive items on the menu, the most costly wines, and then spent the evening complaining about the company and how insensitive leadership was.

Often, we are asked if recognition really works on high-income earners. "Aren't they above this stuff?" someone might ask us. Well, here were the top seven guys in the company—all making a king's ransom in salary—and they were all ticked off because no one cared enough to spend one evening to give them a sincere thanks.

Instead of an evening to celebrate success and achievement, they griped and moaned and tore down the ineffective management of the company. And, of course, they told their friends. That's how we found out.

The word of sincere respect for your employees travels fast. But poor treatment travels at the speed of sound. The devil really is in the details. Pay attention, show up for your top performers, honor them in a way they'll feel is genuine and heartfelt, and they will stay and stay committed. Never forget that it takes people to recognize people.

Through the years, we've found one way to keep recognition real is to recognize what matters most. On the shop floor, it might be no defects. On the loading dock, perhaps it is safety and never-miss delivery. In the hospital newborn intensive care unit, it's accuracy and compassion. In marketing, it might be innovation.

And the reward doesn't have to be dinner in a fancy restaurant in Manhattan. Any manager who has given a handwritten note of thanks—or anyone who has received one—knows the power of the pen. And so, if you do one thing after reading this book, please start mailing a few handwritten notes of thanks. You can buy a stack of thank-you notes online or at any card store. We have seen these types of notes tacked up on walls, pulled out of wallets, hidden in happy files, and kept for years. Why? Because recognition is rare. And because the appreciation is from you, their supervisor. And, most importantly, because it's sincere, noting with specificity something great they've accomplished.

Make It Public

If a tree falls on a mime in a forest, does it make a sound? What about recognition that happens in private? Does it have the same impact?

The answer is, in most cases, no.

At Westfield Group, managers have been trained on the importance of the presentation. Says T. L. Brosseau, manager of operations for this insurance company, "Right after a presentation, you'll see an increase in productivity, and effort and ideas. So as you do a presentation, you always know there is a great tail on the backside of that. This is how we encourage employees to step outside of their box, do something different, and make a difference for Westfield."

And it's working. In the two years since Westfield has enhanced its formal process for recognizing employees, employee satisfaction has increased by a whopping 14 percent. And it was pretty good before then.

According to a survey of more than 33,000 award recipients in the United States and Canada, an effective presentation makes a significant impression. In fact, the presentation of an award affects employees' perception of the company as a whole.

When surveyed employees called an award presentation "excellent," 97 percent of them said their "contribution was acknowledged." Which, of course, is exactly what you want to happen. You want people to feel valued and appreciated. You want them to feel bonded to your organization. But consider what happens when the surveyed employees called their presentation "Poor" or when they had no presentation—receiving their award in the mail. Given those scenarios, only 39 percent of recipients felt their contribution to the company was acknowledged.

Time to hang the "Help Wanted" sign out again.

Now, some might say that any recognition is better than none at all, and we'd agree. But presentation matters. A lot. It's right up there with giving roses on Valentine's Day.

Eric Lang works as a senior leader at VNU Media Measurement Inc. (you know them better as Nielsen Media Research, the TV ratings guys). He related this story to us recently, which the *Wall Street Journal* thought was fantastic enough to be included in an article they wrote on employee recognition.

Before joining VNU, a great firm that gets this stuff, Lang worked at a trucking company that shall remain nameless to protect the guilty. His office pal, we'll call him Paul, was the employee of the year and won the Chairman's Award. To honor the top employee, this trucking company gave the worker a solid gold Presidential Rolex watch.

And while you might be thinking that nothing could mess that up, you'd be wrong. First, the award was presented not by the chairman, not by Paul's boss, but by Brown. That's right, UPS.

One fine morning as Paul came into work he found a package on his desk. In the box was his long-awaited award, the Rolex. No presentation, no kind words, no adoring coworkers or weeping spouse. Not even the green-gilled jealousy of the guy who finished second. Nothing but the hollow sound of phones ringing in the cubicles down the hall.

At about this time, Eric happened on the scene and asked, "What's in the box?" to which Paul replied, "My award. You know . . . the Rolex."

Eric, seeing the disappointment in his eyes, quickly tried to make the moment more memorable. He grabbed up the watch, called in a few coworkers and presented Paul his watch in front of the few people who had arrived early for the day. "Ladies and gentlemen, your Chairman's Award winner—Paul!"

After a few rounds of applause, things seemed to be getting a little better for Paul. But not for long. Eric noticed an envelope that was left behind in the box. Assuming that it must be a letter of congratulations from the chairman, Eric pulled it out and read it.

The value of a Rolex is counted as income. Taxable income. And the letter wasn't from the chairman. It was a 1099 form. It stated that the company had not paid the taxes on the watch and Paul—their number one employee—owed more than $5,000 in income taxes.

When you think about it, this trucking company had sold Paul a gold Rolex for five grand.

And now, the rest of the story. A month later, Eric asked his friend Paul why he never wore the watch.

"Sold it to pay the taxes," was the taciturn reply.

And then, a few months later, Paul tendered his resignation. From No. 1 to gone in just a few months. Why? The bill for taxes owed? That didn't help. The lack of a sincere show of public appreciation? Sure. But worst of all was this: A company full of leaders who didn't understand the need to make a great award presentation to keep a star employee.

Olga Gonzales, now, was a completely different story.

A front-line manager for a utility, she was recently recognized at a management meeting where we were invited to speak.

Before we began, Gonzales's director invited her to the front of the group. He reminded everyone of the challenges they'd be going through with a tough computer system up-grade. He then turned to his report: "I want to recognize Olga for her spirit and for the way she recognizes her team of employees. She exemplifies what we want in our front-line supervisors—setting clear goals and recognizing their performance and really being a positive spirit in the workplace, regardless of all the demands on her during the system conversion."

The leader continued, outlining how Gonzales was making a real difference to her team during a difficult time. And as Gonzales stood there, before the company's top brass, we couldn't help watching her face. It was alive, radiant. We wish you could have seen it. She was still beaming as she left to return to work an hour later. If the director had said the same things to her privately, would it have had the same impact? We doubt it.

Here's another great example from Beverly Gomez, general manager of the Friendly's Restaurant in Hershey, Pennsylvania. We met Gomez in late August, when many of her college student summer staff members were making an exodus back to campus. That left Gomez looking for someone to work the unpopular Saturday shift.

We'll let Gomez tell this story in her own words, unedited.

"I have a server who's been here for 15 years. She has certain days she works. No more, no less. And she never works Saturdays. But I asked her, 'Joan, I know you don't work on Saturdays, but I need a server to work.' She didn't even think about it, she said yes. So I got everyone together. I have a milk crate that I stand on . . . it's my soapbox. So I'm standing on this box, and guests are looking at me. And the employees are saying, 'Who's going to get embarrassed this time?' But even though they complain, they love it. They absolutely love it. They make fun of the person I give the award to, too, but it's friendly ribbing. Anyway, I take out my horn, which is my hand, and I go 'toot, toot, toot, everybody come hither.' Then I give them my little speech about Joan. 'I'm awarding you 4,000 Wow points because I appreciate your team effort. I appreciate you saying yes to working on Saturday without any hesitation.' Everyone laughs at Joan, but something good is happening."

You'd better believe something good is happening. Since Gomez took over the restaurant two years ago, turnover is down 25 percent and the restaurant's financial returns are among the best in Friendly's system.

"I'm kind of a goober about this kind of recognition stuff," adds Gomez. "My employees certainly think I'm a goober and they laugh at me because of it. But that's okay. Because I'm getting the results I want."

Gomez realizes that a major benefit of public recognition that is often overlooked is the impact it has on the people in attendance. They may come for the free donuts—or ice cream in Friendly's case—but employees attending an award celebration will leave with a much better understanding of your teams' priorities and goals.

Sitting there or standing there, watching one of their peers being recognized for supporting one of the company's core values, they can't help but ask themselves, "I wonder what they would say about me?"

Returning to their work, they have a heightened desire to *find out.*

Be Sure It's Appropriate

When it comes to recognition, one size definitely does *not* fit all. Recognition must be personalized to employee interests, needs, and preferences.

Take, for example, the evolving leadership style of Tim Garrett, a senior field manager for DHL's IT processing center. From his Phoenix office, he manages 50 people around the United States for DHL, the world's largest express delivery carrier.

Tim admitted he was becoming the "Coffee Guy" with his employees. For a while, whenever he spotted someone doing something exceptional, he would give that person a gift certificate to a coffee house. Seemed to make sense, right? And none of his employees ever complained. But after reading in one of our books that recognition should be personalized to employee interests, he asked his employees if his style was working.

You can imagine the conversation with a team member:

"You liking those coffee certificates?"

"Well, to be honest, I don't really drink coffee. I give the certificates to my neighbor."

Oops. This well-intentioned manager had been recognizing the employee's neighbor.

"I had to learn that not everyone likes coffee, not everyone likes the same restaurants. They appreciate me making the effort to recognize them. But it goes so much further when I take the time to find out what they like. I'm still learning about the people I work with and what they really value."

As Tim will tell you, coffee certificates may be great for someone who loves the stuff and makes a daily pilgrimage to the ubiquitous green awning of their local coffee house. But for others? It's oops.

Today, this great manager has improved his approach and is learning what's important to his employees. He motivates through personal recognition that is meaningful to his people. And the results—a more engaged and committed workforce that knows their boss is seeing and rewarding above-and-beyond behavior with rewards that are relevant to them.

As Trevor Grams the director of operation services at EPCOR Generation Inc. in Edmonton, Alberta, told us, "When I was plant manager, recognition was more in the form of getting a hat or a t-shirt. . . . When I first became a manager, those were the tools I had in my head. And I quickly discovered they didn't work. I thought I was recognizing people, but I wasn't getting results. I learned I had to personalize things."

Perhaps the most appreciated recognition is that which recognizes and fulfills the personal needs of individual employees. In one touching case, a manager we met had noticed the additional stress of a top employee whose son was having trouble with math in school. She began looking for a chance to recognize her and when that happened, she presented the employee with a certificate for six months of math tutoring for her son—in her home.

In other words, recognition needs to be adapted to each employee. And tied to their needs. This is where a recognition log will come in valuable, helping you to know what an employee will value—and what will make them feel rewarded.

Now, with all this said, awards don't have to be expensive. But they must be perceived as "just," meaning employees accept the award as being appropriate in value to the demands of the job. This can be very subjective—and a little tricky to get right. But, believe us, people will know the instant you've got it wrong. Like the programmers we talked to from a small start-up company.

They initially were pleased when the cash-strapped organization announced a recognition program. But their enthusiasm was short-lived.

"The award for great performance turned out to be a bag of Twizzlers and a star-shaped light—the battery-operated kind that kids buy at an amusement park," said a developer.

The underwhelmed technical employees soon came up with a revealing name for the award: Byte Me.

In our opinion, the story would be dismal enough if it ended right there. But it doesn't. "When I got the award," recalled another developer, "my boss didn't have time to get any Twizzlers. And he told me I could go get the star light from a coworker's desk and put it on mine."

Needless to say, the fellow didn't bother.

Now, there are times for small achievements when a mug or a T-shirt or even a star light would be appropriate and appreciated. At one office we visited, a manager places a wind-up toy genie (out of a McDonald's Happy Meal) on the desk of an employee who has done something great. As the genie moves with a shudder and a jerk around the desk, the boss "grants" the employee one nonmonetary wish: Getting to sleep in and come to work one hour later for a week, a chance to use a carpool car for the weekend, and so on. The boss reports that he's never had to turn down a wish.

Hokey? Sure. Fun? Absolutely. And the employees *love* it.

It's the job of the manager to know their employees well enough to discern what they will value, what will make them feel important. Or, in this case, to let them choose something that will have great impact.

Now, of all the forms of recognition, a symbolic reward has the most lasting impact. These are usually reserved for significant achievements and usually have a greater cost attached. But not always, according to one CEO we know, a former attorney.

"On my desk is a small block of multicolored rock. A pretty ugly paperweight. Why do I keep a laminated lump of shale oil on my desk? For seven years I helped create the synthetic fuels industry in the United States. Only the innermost sanctum of people got this paperweight. It means the world to me. It's a keepsake I will treasure forever."

How could a piece of rock come to mean so much? Because it's symbolic of esteem, respect, and appreciation. In 2002, the whole world watched as a Canadian dollar coin took on the same type of significance for an entire country.

Any Canadian can tell you the story of the country's hockey team president and former hockey great Wayne Gretzky, who dug a dollar coin (a looney) from center ice in Salt Lake City's E Center following Canada's 2002 Olympic Winter Games gold medal victory over the United States.

Now, to understand the significance of this, it's important to know that for millions of Canadians, the Olympic Winter Games aren't a multicultural sporting event. The Olympics are really just a big hockey tournament. Gretzky realized the weight of this challenge in winning the gold and took an important first step when he found a fellow Canadian working at the facility. He conspired to bury the Canadian dollar coin at center ice days before the competition began. Then, he told only his players about the secret under the ice.

What did Gretzky's hidden looney communicate to his players? That Canada owned the ice at the Games. He could have told his players that they should not worry about the United States home advantage—that they had invented this game and had played it longer. He might have reminded them of the superior technical abilities. But he didn't. He simply whispered in the first team meeting of the secret looney buried under center ice, which meant Canada owned the ice. He put substance to the words. And he created a shared experience through a symbol.

Today, that coin is on display, under glass, at the Hockey Hall of Fame in Toronto. It's under glass because when it first opened to the public, folks could touch the coin and it quickly began to lose its features. Everyone wanted to touch the looney for good luck.

Ah, the power of a symbol. A one-dollar coin as valuable as the gold medals it helped the team win.

Here's one last reminder of this, a personal one. When Chester's mother-in-law passed away, his wife Heidi went home to celebrate her mother's life with the family and to support her father. While there, her dad offered each child a chance to pick out something special from among their mother's personal effects to treasure.

As you might guess, there wasn't a lot of fighting over the waffle iron or the vacuum cleaner. Even the stereo and television were left alone. They were all looking for something more symbolic, something personal.

Heidi selected a small statue of a Girl Scout.

There is nothing remarkable about the statue. It isn't made of precious metal. The engraving is simple:

MARION OLSEN 1973

Girl Scouts United States

Heidi's mom had always been a neighborhood chair for the Girl Scouts. "I was just little, but I remember sitting on the floor playing while she was at one of the many meetings for the troop." Of course, in due time, it was Heidi's turn to join the Girl Scouts and continue the tradition her mother helped build. The statue represented not just Girl Scouts but her time with her mom and the service that was the hallmark of her mother's life.

"With that little statue, I will never forget her service to others and those life lessons."

It is not just a small statue of a Girl Scout. It is a mother's memory and a life lesson in service.

Ah yes, there is power in symbols. Whether a family heirloom or the ring that symbolizes 100,000 miles driven without accident, the jacket with the company logo that is only presented on completion of rigorous technical certification, or the crystal apple awarded after an employee receives an advanced degree. These are the things that touch our hearts and engage our emotions. Items that will be passed down to another generation, not sold in a garage sale next spring.

Esteem. Respect. Appreciation. Like the timeless values it communicates, a symbolic award never goes out of style.

Increase the Frequency

"You need breakfast again? Didn't I give you food yesterday?" we often tease our kids. They giggle and guffaw, even though they've heard the joke many times before. Why? Because the whole idea is utterly ridiculous. Everyone knows we need a constant supply of food to keep going.

It's not much different with recognition.

We'll never forget the words of a furniture maker in North Carolina who had just received a recognition award in a sincere, personal ceremony with his coworkers and bosses. He was a charming, straight-talking man. Of his award and its presentation, he said, "It just makes you feel so good. It makes you want to keep on keeping on."

But alas, not forever. Research shows that recognition is most effective when it is given every seven days. It also has more impact when it is given shortly after the achievement.

"Managers, especially new managers, are so caught up in trying to achieve all the things they are trying to do themselves, that sometimes those moments when somebody did something great today are lost," said one manager to us. "A week later telling someone how great they did just doesn't mean as much to you as taking the time today or early tomorrow to let them know, 'That was important to me. That was important to the team and you really made a difference.'"

Informal or day-to-day awards are a great way to keep frequency high. They are more spontaneous and less costly in nature than formal awards. And, yet, done right, they can be some of the most effective recognition moments.

"People are looking for quiet recognition, which means the quiet approval of your boss," says Kevin Wheeler, president of Global Learning Resources, Inc. a Fremont, California, human resources strategist.

Dee Hansford, who headed Disney World Corporation's employee recognition program in the mid-1990s, was known to spontaneously appear throughout the park to give recognition. She would walk through the kitchen of a restaurant at the theme park and comment how it sparkled and how Disney's rating with the health board would go through the roof.

In 1995, with no additional employees hired, cast members handled 15 percent more guests at the theme park, received no pay increases or bonuses and still increased their job satisfaction by 15 percentage points.

Guest satisfaction and "interest-to-return" survey scores also were "incredibly high." Moreover, Disney's annual report showed a 15 percent increase in revenues directly attributed to the theme park that year.

Simple, specific praise can have a remarkable impact. And, as we've noted, there are many times when a personal note can be the very best recognition. We both travel frequently. Early on in our visits, we make it a point to leave a note for the chambermaid (along with a tip), telling her how nice it is to return to such a meticulous, well-kept room. We have always received a nice note in return—and often extra chocolates, to boot.

Notes have made a huge impact at Baltimore-based financial services company T. Rowe Price, too. Entering the building, a visitor can't help but notice all the thank-you cards and e-mails papering employee workspaces—40,000 in the first year after the company's Spotlight Program was introduced, said Sharon Gilbert, vice president of client communications.

The Spotlight Program encourages employees and leaders to send "Spotlight cards" to employees in recognition of above-and-beyond performance in the areas of Service, Teamwork,

Leadership or Innovation, the company's core values.

"We want to reinforce the behaviors we want repeated . . . and it is working. We have seen our client [satisfaction] scores go up. And associates are just happier and feel more appreciated," said Gilbert.

Perhaps most revealing, after one year, employees gave the Spotlight program a 92 percent approval rating. How many of your HR programs have that high a level of satisfaction?

Another time, believe it or not, the best spontaneous, informal reward turned out to be a stuffed carrot.

It was the last of four days of training in Beijing, China, in 2005. And I [Chester] was seated in a very familiar restaurant. Each day, all the teachers and our students from a management class had gathered at the same eatery—and each day I had been assisted by the same server. My glass was always full. She expertly helped me navigate the unfamiliar menu. And she always had a smile on her face.

So, during my last lunch in Beijing, I decided to return the favor. Near the end of my meal, I called her over to say thanks for the great service. I explained to her (through my interpreter) that in my company we recognize and reward outstanding service. She immediately brightened and said, "Well, I want to work for you, then." I went on to explain that we call it the "Power of the Carrot," and to commemorate her great service I presented her with a "Garrett the Carrot."

Now, Garrett is a plush, smiling carrot. They cost a couple of dollars to make and (you guessed it) they make them in China. An inexpensive gift to be sure, but to our server it was like receiving an Academy Award. She called her friends over and we took many pictures. For the rest of the lunch hour she was a superstar: the most valued, appreciated, and productive server in the restaurant. And all because of a stuffed carrot and a simple *Xie Xie* (thank you).

Amazing what a little thanks can do.

---

50 Ways to Recognize

Ever found yourself with a case of "thanker's block?" Not to worry, it happens to the best of us. Luckily, we've discovered that there are as many ways to provide recognition as there are people to recognize. More, actually. And that's what makes recognition fun: It is limited only by your imagination. So, to help get your creative juices flowing, we've compiled 50 fun ways to recognize your best and brightest.

For personal achievement:

- During a recognition ceremony, give an employee a bouquet of flowers—one at a time. With each flower, express thanks for a specific achievement.

- Assign an employee to work on the most exciting, visible project in the company. Sometimes opportunity is the greatest award.

- Invite an employee to join you for lunch with your boss. Introduce him well and describe his recent achievements.

- Create a funny traveling trophy—like a tiara, rubber chicken, or GI Joe doll (you da' man! award)—and pass it around to the great performer of the week.

- Clean the snow off an employee's car and get it heated up before she leaves the office on a snowy workday.

- Put a wind-up toy genie on an achiever's desk and grant them one nonmonetary wish.

- Give an employee a garden statue for her new yard (with an inscription that reminds her how your appreciation continues to "grow").

- Buy children's party decorations (in the child's favorite theme) for an employee who is too busy to plan the child's birthday party herself.

- Upgrade an employee's work area with a new chair or computer equipment.

- Pay an employee's parking fees for a month or even a year.

- Bring in a shoeshine guy or manicurist to pamper an employee at her desk.

- Provide a limo ride to and from work.

- Arrange for an employee's favorite local celebrity to visit his desk and present a fun award.

- Provide valet parking at the door of the office building for a star. (Don't forget to put up a sign reading "Valet Parking for _____.")

- Bring in a violinist to serenade an employee at her desk for a few minutes.

- Pay for a crew to rake an employee's leaves or clear the snow from his driveway.

- Provide a personal chef to cook dinner in an employee's home for a week.

- Give the gift of a family portrait.

- Commission an amusing song or poem especially for an employee.

- Upgrade an employee's next airline trip to first class. When she's on her way to the airport, leave her a voice mail explaining what you've done and why (and watch her commitment level soar).

- Fly him to his next out-of-town meeting on the corporate jet.

- For an animal lover, let him bring his pet to work for a day (make sure no one's allergic beforehand).

- When you win a huge deal—say, for a million dollars—frame a copy of the check in a wide, white frame and sign it, "You were a huge part of this."

- Hire someone to hang up—and take down—an employee's outdoor holiday lights (you provide the lights).

- When an employee travels to a cool city for business, invite him to add an extra day of rest and relaxation—on you.

- Give an employee a photo of the team framed in a wide, white mat frame. Have team members sign the mat with a personal, congratulatory note.

- Plan a fun medal ceremony on a riser for a top performer. Include humorous pomp and circumstance. The gesture will be light, but the thought sincere.

- Send a book to an employee's child on the child's birthday. Sign the inside cover with, "Your mom is so cool around here."

- Give an employee a sleep-in pass for two hours when he is getting stressed. Wouldn't it be great not to set the alarm for a day?

- When an employee is working outside on a hot day, find out what his favorite non-alcoholic drink is, and deliver a huge, cold one. Nothing says thanks like a Big Gulp.

- Send a fruit basket to an employee's home. Don't forget to include a handwritten, specific note of thanks. (His family will thank him, too.)

- At holiday time, give an employee two hours off at lunch to buy gifts or to go home early.

- Give an employee a print by his favorite artist.

- Offer to be an employee's assistant for a day, helping him get the job done.

- When an employee travels on business, get her a ticket to the "big show" in town (i.e., in New York, get her a Broadway ticket).

- Allow an employee and his family to use the corporate suite during a sporting or music event.

- Pay for an employee's pet care while he or she is out of town on business.

- Give a pet lover a new fancy collar for his best friend or a gift certificate for a free pet grooming.

- As a team, do an employee's yard work while he is at work or on a trip. It's amazing what an hour (of service) can do for an employee's commitment level.

- When an employee moves to bigger and better responsibility in your company, create a momento, like a small statue for her office.

- Print up a simple "Hall Pass" that lets an employee leave work at noon.

- In this technological world, the most memorable gift may be organic—flower bulbs, seeds, or a tree.

- Give a makeover or a manicure.

- Send an employee on a river-rafting trip.

- Take the driving enthusiast on a test-drive of a Ferrari or other exotic car. Vroom! Vroom!

- Arrange for a golfer to play an exclusive course—at home or on a business trip.

- Send a skier to her favorite resort for the day—all expenses paid.

- Send an employee to NASCAR driver's school or a fantasy sports camp.

- Give a day of labor from the whole team to a star employee's favorite charity.

For team successes:

- Schedule a foosball or ping-pong tournament for a Friday.

- Host a department casino night. Everyone gets chips and the winners turn them in at the end of the night for prizes.

- Take the group kite flying.

- Throw a pizza party at lunch. Who doesn't love a party?

- Take everyone to a movie on Friday afternoon. Believe us, Denzel's latest blockbuster is even better when you see it on company time.

- Invite everyone to an all-day mandatory meeting—after a stressful stretch at work—at a day spa.

- Hire a clean comedian to entertain the group over box lunches.

- Take everyone skating—roller or ice. You rent the equipment and pay the entry.
- Buy a bunch of customized henna tattoos with your company logo and a fun tagline.
- Bring in motorized racecars and have a race. The winner gets a prize. But everyone takes home their cars.
- Hire a fortune teller to tell (happy) fortunes.
- Host an Olympic day complete with obstacle courses, timed events, no-gravity boots and fun physical events.
- Go out and build a snowman together.
- Bring in a mariachi band to play during lunch.
- On Halloween, bring in masks and wigs for everyone. Whoever gets the mullet wig has to wear it all day.
- On a hot day working outside, bring the group ice-cream sandwiches.
- Make the workplace more comfortable, based on the group's suggestions.
- Rent a popcorn machine and hand out all-you-can-eat popcorn all afternoon.
- Greet employees in the morning with designer coffees—on the house.
- Hire a barbeque or taco stand to serve lunch to everyone.
- Make the most of formal recognition awards. Gather everyone in the group together whenever you present service, performance, and sales awards.

(Okay, so we couldn't resist—that was 70. But that's the way it is with recognition: Once you get started, it's hard to stop. And why would you want to?)

For 365 more ideas, we'd recommend keeping a copy of *A Carrot a Day* around the office. Just read one a day, and you'll become a better leader with never-ending ideas for rewarding your employees.

VISIBLE TOOL

A Message in an e-Bottle

Right now, before you turn another page, think of someone on your team who deserves recognition for an above-and-beyond behavior, and send them an e-card of thanks.

Tie your message to a specific core value that is important to your team. Make it specific—explain exactly what the employee did that was outstanding and moved you closer to your team goals. And then, before you forget or have second thoughts—hit send.

Here's a sample e-mail: "Dear Amy, I just wanted to thank for stepping in on the monthly tallies. As you know, Ty was buried with consolidations, and I don't know how we would have got the month-ends done without your help. You showed excellent Teamwork, which as you know, is one of our core goals around here. Thanks again!"

Pretty simple, huh? So, let's get started. You can send a free e-mail card from one of our favorite sites, **thanks.com**, or just send a regular e-mail. The important thing is to give thanks.

Do it regularly, and your employees will begin thanking you back—with improved performance and morale.

CHAPTER FIVE

Visible Results

In no time at all, it seemed to Ian, it was the Fruits of the Laborer ceremony again. As he dressed in his ceremonial robes, Ian's mind raced. This would not be like any ceremony before—and hopefully there would never be one like it again.

But Ian was the only one, it seemed, with any tension on this special night. All around him, people went about their normal routines, preparing without much interest for the gems they would reap during the evening's festivities.

Together, the Highlanders hoisted the obligatory baskets filled with fruits and grains and vegetables onto their shoulders and walked to the foothills of the first mountain. Before entering the clearing, they stopped to arrange their procession, the thick underbrush hiding them and the place of offering from view. People whispered to each other as they adjusted their baskets. Someone behind Ian straightened a rucksack.

Suddenly, the drums began and the chief elder pushed through the trees and entered the clearing. Then he stopped abruptly. The Highlanders immediately behind him bumped into each other. Baskets were jostled and a few tumbled to the ground. The drums missed a beat, then slowly trailed off as one by one the Highlanders entered the clearing. And stopped, incredulous.

There was nothing in the chests.

Nothing but a small handful of broken stones in the bottom of one box. The rest were empty. The wind blew up a dust devil and a hinge on a chest lid squeaked. For a moment, every eye watched the small cyclone whip wildly over the hillside.

The sound of a loud voice made them start.

It was the chief elder as he pushed past the Highlanders responsible for this mountain. "Okay, folks. Nothing to worry about. Plenty of mountains to get to today. Let's just head to the next place of offering."

In encouragement, the drummers started up and played with enthusiasm all the way there. The hopeful mood was contagious and people began to anticipate the harvest. That is, until they stepped into another empty clearing. And found nothing again but the almost-empty chests.

And so it continued on hillside after hillside all throughout the evening hours.

By the time the Highlanders arrived at the farthest mountain, they were terrified. They entered without pomp or circumstance, in groups of two or three—and stopped, astounded by what they saw.

They had expected nothing. But instead found a clearing filled with brimming chests of rubies and sapphires—and emeralds. Gems were even piled on the ground and stacked in barrels, indicating the harvest had been too great to fit in the chests.

"What is going on here!" demanded the chief of the elders. He was out of breath and pounded his walking stick on the ground. He had been the last to arrive in the field. Now he pushed forward in anger and confusion. Then stopped, stunned by the sight that met his eyes. He turned back, his eyes searching the crowd.

"Whose mountain is this?"

"It's Ian's," someone muttered, and the elder spun to look for the young man.

"Ian! Where are you!" he demanded.

Ian pushed to the front of the Highlanders.

"There you are. I...What did...How did you..." the elder asked, motioning wildly toward the piles of jewels behind his back.

"I didn't," said Ian, softly.

The chief's eyes narrowed.

"*We* did," Ian said. He smiled as he stared fixedly at the jewels behind the chief's back.

Several of the Highlanders gasped.

Hearing them, the chief didn't turn immediately, as if afraid of what he might see. When he did, he could scarcely believe his eyes. There among the jewels were...But could he trust his vision?...Were they? The Invisible People?

Ian walked past him to stand at the front of the group, next to Star.

"These are the Wurc-Urs in my care," said Ian, motioning to the silent people standing amid the chests. "And this is one of our most talented, Star."

She smiled at Ian.

"The Wurc-Urs have suffered, unnoticed," he continued. "But these people need to be seen. We need them to be seen if we are all to succeed. Without them, we will *all* disappear."

Ian watched as the leader's eyes raced from him to the Wurc-Urs to the riches littering the ground. Ian had dreamed of this moment—envisioned himself standing here triumphantly at the front of the Wurc-Urs. But now he realized that something was wrong with that picture. And he understood why. He hesitated only a moment. And then walked to stand *behind* the Wurc-Urs.

A hum of excited voices filled the air. Tentatively, a few Highlanders moved forward to inspect the flawless gems. A few of the Invisible People joined them and there began a few awkward conversations.

And standing there, behind the Wurc-Urs, was Ian; who suddenly had the strange sensation that he had never, ever, been so *visible*.

VISIBLE RESULTS

The ROI (and ROE and ROA) of Visibility

Wouldn't it be great if a single business strategy allowed you to meet your business objectives simultaneously? Well, this must be your lucky day. Here's how it works: *Customer loyalty* and *investor loyalty* are all founded on *employee commitment and loyalty,* which triggers *high-level performance.* And what improves employee commitment and loyalty? *Employee recognition.*

And it all begins with a leader who is willing to put his or her workers first—and stand behind them, letting them bask in the glow of recognition.

Marcus Buckingham, author of *The One Thing You Need to Know,* explained it this way, "Good managers don't need reminding of the power of praise. They seem to know instinctively that praise isn't merely a reaction to great performance; it is the cause of it."

Something amazing happens when employees see managers using their valuable time and effort to honor them. It touches their egos. (Let's be honest, who doesn't like to be recognized?) More than that, it creates a "shared moment." This "shared moment" of mutual respect builds an emotional connection between the company, manager, and employee. Because of that connection, the employee engages and commits to the work at hand, and is willing to do more than put in time. That strengthens the corporate culture and enables managers to deliver more to the company through the efforts of the people who actually do the work—the employees. In short, you create an engaged workforce.

So, what does an *engaged* employee look like, exactly? It has nothing to do with a gold ring, but everything to do with attitude. Engaged workers care about the quality of their work and their companies—and they enjoy what they are doing. But perhaps the easiest way to recognize an engaged workforce is by taking a look at the company's long-term bottom line.

According to Hewitt's work on employee engagement, "Engagement is highly correlated to key business measures, including productivity and retention, customer satisfaction, total shareholder return (TSR) and sales growth. Organizations that have improved their engagement level have realized corresponding improvements in their business success measures."

In their book, *Giving Employees What They Want: The Returns Are Huge,* Louis A. Mischkind and Michael Irwin Meltzer recount the finding of a survey by Sirota Consulting. Out of 28 companies in the study, 14 of those firms—the ones considered to have a high morale—saw their stock prices increase an average of 16 percent in 2004 alone. The industry average for the year was 6 percent. And six "low morale" companies increased an average of just 3 percent.

But perhaps the most compelling link between recognition and the bottom-line results came in 2005. In a survey of 26,000 employees at all levels in 31 organizations, The Jackson Organization found direct correlations between recognition and operating margin, return on equity and return on assets.

Companies that employees' ranked in the lowest quartile of agreement with the statement, "My organization recognizes excellence," saw just a 2.4 percent annual return on equity (ROE). In contrast, companies where employees ranked management highest on that important question experienced an 8.7 percent ROE. In other words, organizations that effectively recognize excellence enjoyed a return more than triple the ROE of companies that don't.

But that's just scratching the surface. An equivalent connection was shown on the Jackson study between recognition and return on assets (ROA). Companies that effectively recognize excellence enjoyed an ROA more than three times higher than the return experienced by companies that don't. Since ROA is a measurement of a firm's effectiveness in using the assets at hand to generate earnings, organizations who recognize employee excellence can do a lot more with what they've got than those who neglect this important tool.

In general, companies with higher operating margins tend to have lower fixed costs and better gross margins, which gives them more pricing flexibility and an added measure of safety during tough economic times. And what the researchers found is that of all the financial measures, employee recognition perhaps impacts operating margin the most significantly. According to the data, companies with employees in the highest quartile of agreement with the statement, "My organization recognizes excellence" reported an operating margin of 6.6 percent, while those in the lowest quartile were at a meager 1 percent.

That's a lot of numbers, but behind them are more engaged, productive employees.

Why do we share this? To help you justify spending a few bucks on recognition with the senior management of your firm. For a PDF of The Jackson Group discovery white paper to download in PowerPoint format, go to **invisibleemployee.com** and click on Research.

You know, your gut instinct probably has told you all along that recognition impacts the bottom line. Now you have the data to back it up.

CHAPTER SIX

Blink *Backs*

The next morning, Ian rubbed the sleep from his eyes as he waited for the other caretakers to join him at the base of his mountain. Last night the music and dancing and celebrations had lasted for hours. Today, he knew, there would be many questions from the caretakers.

He waited until the sun was directly overhead before going to look for them. He found them at the observation tower, staring half-heartedly through telescopes at their empty mountains.

"What in the world are you doing?" Ian asked. "I've been waiting at the foot of the mountain for hours. The workers were ready to return with you to your mountains. What happened?"

They turned to face him, but no one answered.

And then it hit him. They simply didn't know what to do next.

"Listen. Come with me." He looked at their worried faces. "Trust me," he said, then turned to lead the way to Sakas Mountain.

As luck would have it, the first Wurc-Ur they met there was Tup—one of the truly committed. He was emptying a bag of rubies gently into a chest at the foot of the mountain. The caretakers stared.

"How is the new pulley system working?" asked Ian, glancing at the ropes overhead.

Tup gave him a thumbs-up.

Ian turned to the caretakers and said, "It's a new method. Been running just a couple of days. Tup was the one who suggested installing it. This way, Wurc-Urs can focus on collecting jewels—and not waste so much time on trips up and down. They get up on the mountain in the morning and stay there until dinner."

As he spoke, a bag slid down the line toward them. Tup caught it and took it off the line. He gently poured the red and blue and purple stones into the chest.

"Thanks to Tup and this pulley, we get very few broken stones now," said Ian. "So the quality is up. And our workers are happier with fewer trips up and down, which is safer for the workers. And we bring down more gems in a day. Those are our goals, you know: satisfied and safe Wurc-Urs, higher quality, greater volume."

He caught a look at Tup's face. It was glowing with pride.

"So how does it work?" asked a caretaker suddenly. Ian jumped slightly. It was the first time a caretaker had spoken that day.

"Tup, why don't you show them?" asked Ian.

The caretakers listened intently as Tup described the system. He then led them slowly up the mountain, explaining each step in the process.

At the end of the day the caretakers returned, hot, tired—and eager to begin this process on their own mountains.

Over the campfire that night, Ian introduced the Wurc-Urs from each mountain to their supervisors.

As the fire died down, the Wurc-Urs returned to their homes, but the supervisors remained...as if waiting for something. Ian knew what it was.

"Once you have *SET* your goals together, the next step is to *SEE*."

Ian smiled at their raised eyebrows and walked into the darkness toward home.

The next morning, Ian went to the observation tower first, afraid that he might find the caretakers huddled there again. But, to his relief, the platform was empty.

He set out for the first mountain, finding the caretaker on the path, walking with a Wurc-Ur.

"I never realized how steep this path is. It's not the most direct route, either," explained the caretaker. "We were talking about our goals this morning and the Wurc-Urs showed me a less-used path that would be much faster and easier. It'll take some time...we'll need to widen it and improve it. But the payoff could be large. That would make the Wurc-Urs more satisfied and increase our volume. Kendall here suggested it."

"Great," said Ian. "You're *seeing* already. The next step is to recognize Kendall's idea. Find a way to celebrate this win tonight."

"The new path?" asked the caretaker. "But we haven't built it yet."

"You are recognizing the idea, not the implementation," Ian patiently explained. "That's another celebration for another day."

Ian smiled and set off for the next mountain. At each, he found tired and winded caretakers on the trails—looking hopeful.

It was late in the day when Ian reached the second-to-last mountain. It was, beyond a doubt, the most challenging, with jagged cliffs and steep drop-offs. The caretaker's face fell when he mentioned a celebration. "I can't think of a thing to celebrate. It hasn't been an easy day for anyone," she admitted.

"Of course, you won't have a celebration every day. But you just finished your first day together as a team—I'd celebrate that," suggested Ian. "Celebrations have a way of creating more reasons to celebrate. And anyway, when it seems like there's nothing to celebrate, that's when your team needs it more than ever."

As he walked away, Ian wondered if the discouraged Highlander would take his advice. He hoped she would.

That night, Ian left his own group's gathering for a few moments to listen for sounds around the mountain. He could hear sporadic bursts of cheering and laughter throughout the valley. Best of all, he could see a large bonfire and hear music coming from the tall, jagged mountain closest to his, which had nothing to celebrate except a safe first day together.

It was a good sign. He couldn't wait for morning. Or the next. Or the one after that.

∞

After that first night of celebration, things on Mediokr Island seemed to get better and better. The Wurc-Urs were regularly harvesting emeralds now—on all the mountains. The work was easier and more rewarding—and the harvest was larger and of better quality than ever before. The Wurc-Urs and the Highlanders were working so closely now it was often difficult to tell them apart. Everyone was treated with respect. Everyone was listened to. Great work was celebrated. Best of all, there had been no Blink Outs now for a very long time.

And the treasure grew.

On the one-year anniversary of the shocking—and now historic—Fruit of the Laborer ceremony, the Highlanders and Wurc-Urs planned a grand celebration of the dramatic changes. Toward the end of the evening, Ian climbed on a large rock surrounded by hundreds of baskets of glistening, jewel-colored fruit and called for quiet. The drums stopped and the crowd fell silent.

"In the past year, we have accomplished what we set out to do," said Ian. The people cheered. "But I have heard you talking. You're talking about diamonds. You're saying we should be bringing them down again. It was done years ago. It can be done now. Together, this year, we can bring down the first diamonds in more than a decade!"

The drums and cheers were deafening. Ian jumped down from the rock, landing near Star.

She was smiling, but there was a look in her eyes. He knew what it was.

"We could sure use Jon right now, huh?" he said. She nodded.

Suddenly, the air around Ian felt heavy with electricity. For a moment, he worried that he himself was about to Blink Out. He heard a small pop and suddenly, *incredibly,* a man materialized out of nowhere. Ian recognized him instantly.

It was Jon.

Ian heard Star cry out in surprise and saw her run to embrace Jon. Others Wurc-Urs followed, creating a scene of ecstatic chaos.

∞

"We thought you were dead," said Star, weeping with joy. "Where have you been?"

He laughed. "Nope. Not dead. But... I did go to a place where I was needed. Now, it looks like the best place to be is here."

He caught Ian's eye above the crowd. "The word about Kopani is spreading fast. I'd wager I won't be the only Wurc-Ur to Blink Back."

And he was right. After Jon, many other Wurc-Urs blinked back. They had heard of the changes and success of the island and returned to be a part of it. Jon brought down the first diamond in many years and helped countless others— like Star, Remi, and Tup—to reach the same heights.

∞

Even now, in candlelight and around campfires, Wurc-Urs and Highlanders alike recount the legend of the See-er—and how his vision saved the people of Kopani.

"Today, we work together for success," says the elder. "It is hard to believe now that it has ever been any other way."

Sometimes a youngster, busily poking the fire with a stick, will look up at this point and ask, "But aren't we *really* in charge of the Wurc-Urs? We're the bosses, right?"

And around the campfire, the eyes of the old Highlanders suddenly cloud as if they are seeing another—frightening—time.

"It's just better when we work together," says the chief elder, gently but firmly.

And always a small child, glancing nervously around the room at the dancing shadows, asks, "Will anyone ever be invisible again?"

"Never," the elder always answers. "It is the way."

BLINK BACKS

What Do They Expect?

You might have heard the story of the star salesperson who was killed in a tragic accident with a handheld garlic press. (Don't ask.) When he arrived at the Pearly Gates, St. Peter greeted him with the following news: "You must spend one day in Heaven and one day in Hell before choosing where to spend eternity."

The first day was to be spent in Hell. But instead of the general weeping and wailing and gnashing of teeth that he expected, the salesman found himself in a beautiful setting, eating delicious food, and talking to fascinating people who seemed impressed and fascinated with his background. He had such a good time, he found he didn't want to leave when the day was over.

After his surprising experience with Hell, he was a little nervous about what Heaven would look like. (*Was it opposite day in the afterlife?* he worried.) But as it turned out, Heaven was nice, too, with harp music and lots of fluffy, white clouds, just as expected.

It was a tough decision. But in the end the salesman chose to spend eternity in Hell. It was just a little more edgy than Heaven, he reasoned.

When he got there, however, he found it changed beyond recognition. Deflated-looking people wandered hopelessly across a scorching desert, doing meaningless, never-ending tasks.

"What's happened?" he cried out to the Devil. "Just two days ago I was here at a fantastic party with fascinating people. Now, everyone is miserable and the conditions are intolerable."

The Devil cast him a knowing smile. "Oh," he said. "That was recruiting day. Now you're an *employee.*"

When we've told that story, people give us the same look. It says: That would be quite funny—if it wasn't so sad. Sad but *true.*

The picture employees get before they join a company—during the interview process—is often dramatically different from day-to-day life. And the biggest difference is the interpersonal relationship between the supervisor and the employee.

Consider this: During the interview process, a potential employee has her supervisor's full and undivided attention. Her achievements are listed and discussed—at length. She is asked about her career and five-year goals. She is encouraged to ask questions. In other words, she's listened to, respected, valued, and recognized for what she's done in the past. And then she is hired.

And . . . all too often . . . everything changes.

Take Jeff, who signed on to his dream job— only to find himself in his worst nightmare.

"I got there on the first day and couldn't believe it," he said. "No one was expecting me. My supervisor was on vacation. They didn't have a desk cleaned out for me, so I cleaned it out myself . . . and, uh, basically waited for my boss to get back. No one really knew what to do with me. Those were the five longest days of my career."

In fact, it got worse. Even when the supervisor returned, he didn't see her for another week.

"No kidding. Written instructions were left on my desk or given to me through a coworker or e-mail or voice mail. I finally got to see her again at the monthly staff meeting. She looked at me like nothing had happened and said, 'Welcome to the company!' I figured I might never see her again for another month, so I handed over my two-week notice right then."

Remarkably, the story doesn't end there. Jeff's supervisor took immediate action. She met with him. Listened to his frustrations and concerns. *Made changes.* And, remarkably, Jeff stayed.

"I figured that if I had a supervisor that was really willing to continually improve, who would listen and do something about what I said, and then give me the recognition I needed, well, that was unusual. It meant a lot."

And he's not alone. In a recent survey by the Nierenberg Group and New York University's Management Institute, working professionals were asked what would make them reconsider staying at a job that they planned to leave. They responded:

- More opportunities for advancement
- Increase in salary and benefits
- Better recognition for contributions

And, hey, with a boss who Sees and Celebrates, who needs golden handcuffs?

The Power of Change

The secret, of course, is change. Changing your office so that it really is the place employees thought it was when they hired on. Changing the way all your leaders work with employees. Transforming your organization into a place people never want to leave. And, if they've already gone, a place they line up to return to.

Yes, you can create your own Blink Backs.

The bottom line is, you must create an environment where employees are treated as contributing, important members of the team—as grown-ups, not as children who must be led by the hand; and certainly not as foes who must be controlled. Just about everyone shows up at work wanting to give their best and hoping to take pride in their accomplishments. But commitment dies when we find ourselves timed during bathroom breaks, searched at the doors, or ignored after our contributions.

In the best organizations and teams, management sees and celebrates the fact that it's the employees who are getting the work done. Managers are trained to listen to each employee and treat each person uniquely. And in turn, employees feel engaged, committed, and loyal.

But, as you read this, if you feel at a loss as to how to build that kind of organization, you're not alone. Most leaders weren't really trained to do any of this. In our work with managers around the world, many sheepishly admit they really don't know how to motivate the employees they supervise.

So how did they become managers in the first place? By being the best machinist on the factory floor, or the lab tech that had been there the longest, or the engineer who also had an MBA. Now, do any of those things qualify you to lead and motivate people? No more than having driver's licenses qualifies us to drive a New York City subway train.

As Bill Newby, managing director of enterprise process management for Xcel Energy, said, "About a year ago, we recognized a gap—people get promoted because of what they do, not because they are good managers. That means we need to give them the tools, training, and encouragement they need to become good managers. . . ."

That's spot on. Every good manager has to have the right tools for his trade.

The Importance of Training

And just what is a manager's trade?

When it comes right down to it, the most important thing a manager can do—ahead of budgets, technology concerns, introducing new products or services, or even pleasing the head office—is to focus on their people and their contributions.

O. C. Tanner CEO Kent Murdock had this epiphany not long after taking the helm of his worldwide firm.

"It took me a while to figure out what it meant to be a leader. I spent the first few years concentrating on budgets and strategy and technology until I realized that the single most important thing I (and every leader) must do is to focus on the people and creating the right culture, of recognition, for them," he said.

We're not surprised, really. Because in our minds—and those of many others—leadership isn't so much about tricks of the trade or "acting" like a manager. Rather, it's the natural outcome of a sincere relationship of mutual respect between employees and supervisors. A relationship that includes regular, sincere recognition. It's this relationship that fosters long-term sustainable results.

"If you don't reinforce the right behaviors, you don't have recognition programs, you don't run an employee suggestion scheme, how on earth do you expect to [transform your business]?" asked Bill Newby of Xcel Energy. "You can do it, but it won't stick. Strategic recognition is about the stickiness of that transformation."

Why, then, is so much leadership training focused on everything but recognition?

Somewhere along the way, we got way off track. We began to see management as the ability to crunch numbers and manage complex projects and compose flow charts. North American businesses began to expend billions of dollars each year on executive training, much of it heavily focused on leadership skills. Ironically, many of these executive training expenditures have yielded very low rates of return on investment for their corporate sponsors—and leadership knows it.

There's another reason that we neglect recognition training—even in companies where they believe in it. It's because senior management thinks it should happen naturally, like . . . breathing and growing hair.

The funny thing is, there aren't many other things that do come naturally to us human beings. Not eating solid food, not sleeping through the night, not talking, writing, riding a bike—not walking or sitting, for that matter. Like most skills, recognition must be learned. And it's rarely picked up through on-the-job experience—even 15 years of it.

You see, length of time on the job is never a fair indicator of management skill and ability. Stephen P. Robbins, author of *The Truth About Managing People,* explained it this way: "Too often, 20 years of experience is nothing other than 1 year of experience repeated 20 times."

When it comes right down to it, the only real measure of management success is the ability to create a culture where people can succeed. A culture where they feel valued and want to stay. In other words, a *recognition* culture.

And a leader's first step to creating that recognition culture is recognizing his or her own need for recognition training. In his book, *The Choice Is Yours,* John C. Maxwell named one of the chapters "Growth Is a Choice." We love that. It's like a sermon in just four words. *Growth is a choice.*

And that's the point of recognition training. It's a choice that will take you to the next level. It creates tension between where we are and where we need to be. It gives managers the knowledge they need to heat up their departments—and set their employees on fire.

Not so long ago, we received a note from a woman who had been obligated to attended one of our presentations at her company. She admitted that she had been skeptical about coming to a "recognition training" event. But then, during the presentation, something had been said that changed her mind—and her management technique—forever.

"You mentioned that sometimes the most important time to celebrate is when it appears that there is *nothing* worthy of celebration. That's completely counter-intuitive, but somehow it made sense. And I think it helped bring us out of a slump. I've been to hundreds of training events over the past 23 years, but none as impactful as this one. I just wanted to say thank you for your real life, practical advice."

After that final sentence she added parenthetically, "See, I've learned to recognize people for their contributions in a specific way!"

And so can every manager, who makes the conscious choice . . . *to grow.*

Succeed!

Recall for a moment the story of Adrian's dad, Gordon Gostick, the young Rolls-Royce draftsman. His words speak volumes. Of his role at that fine company some 50 years ago, he said:

"I knew what was expected of me."	**Set**
"Managers were trained to listen to employees."	**See**
"My name was on the drawing."	**Celebrate**

And, he "enjoyed every day," which is success. Why?

Gordon called us back a few days after we told him his story would be in this book. "I've been thinking about this a bit more," he added. "It comes down to this: If you don't have an interest in your job, it doesn't matter how much you get paid, you don't want to get up in the morning."

We guess father really did know best. (By the way, thanks, Dad.)

The secret to engaged employees and a successful workplace is in a company full of people who get up in the morning and throw their fist in the air and say, "Yes, I get to go in to work today." And that can be created with a focus on just three words: Set, See, and Celebrate. And when you focus on those, Success is not far behind.

So again, why would we call a workforce that enjoys coming to work every day a success? Because 56 million jobs will open before the year 2012. As the founder of the online job marketplace Monster said, "You think 1999 was a bad time to be hiring? That year was only a footprint for what we'll see in 2008. We'll be facing the worst labor shortage in our lifetime within the next five years."

Better hold on tight . . . to your employees. Better yet, you better recognize them.

Remember, early in the book, how we talked about the process triggered by a manager recognizing an employee. How it created a shared moment. And how that shared moment created a bond with the leader and the company—and how the employee was energized to create future results. Well, Harryette Johnson, Xcel Energy's corporate business unit pricing consultant, knows just how that feels:

"Once you get recognized, you can move the earth for the company. You really feel like you're beaming a little higher at that moment. It's very meaningful. For me, the recognition and the feeling in our group is one of the things that helps me get up in the morning. It's a real collaborative effort to strive for a good bottom line. There is an underlying respect that accompanies recognition that the team grows off of."

Here's one last simple example of this entire process that hit home for us recently. Scott Christopher is one of our favorite recognition trainers. He knows that our clients are king, since we *set* pretty simple goals around here. Then, we had a chance to *see* something pretty amazing. Scott arrived late one Sunday night at the Cincinnati airport for a connection into Buffalo. He was supposed to train at Rich's Foods the next morning, and yet he found himself at the gate looking at a flight-cancelled notice.

"We have you on a flight to Buffalo on Tuesday," said the helpful gate attendant.

"Tuesday? I'm presenting at 8 A.M. tomorrow morning. Tomorrow is Monday," Scott reminded the woman.

She clicked on her keyboard for a few minutes until she admitted there was nothing she could do.

Instead of calling it a day . . . or night . . . Scott grabbed a map of the Eastern United States. Buffalo was just three inches away from Cincinnati. He could probably drive that far.

So without even thinking it out, or calling one of us, he jumped into the last rental car available and drove all night through a blizzard to Buffalo. He arrived at his hotel at 6:30 A.M., showered and shaved, and was picked up at 7.

On stage that morning, Scott absolutely killed them. We're not just saying that because he works for us, Scott is a former stand-up comedian and has no parallel as a trainer. He's funny, engaging, and always relevant. (Are we being specific in our praise, or what?) And then, instead of sleeping for a few hours, Scott got back in his rental car and returned it to Cincinnati—eight hours away—since it was due back at the same airport that day.

Now, did we *celebrate?* You better believe it. We were so blown away by his heroics that Scott received not one but two formal awards in front of our entire team for his dedication to our clients and his innovation.

And best of all, his example taught an old dog how to behave. When Chester's late flight was cancelled getting into Rochester a few months later, he knew what to do. He got in a rental car and drove through the night to make it. Scott Christopher had shown the way in customer heroics, and had let everyone know the kind of behavior we rewarded.

Can you *see* it? The power of employee recognition? We are passionate that every manager must. Because once you do, nothing can stop you.

So, are you ready? On your mark . . . Set! See! Celebrate!

And *succeed*.

NOTES

Introduction

Page xiii "In his book, *Achieving Total Quality,* . . ." Wayne H. Brunetti, *Achieving Total Quality* (White Plains, NY: Quality Resources, 1993).

Page xiv "Only 4 percent of the 90,000 people . . ." Kristine Ellis, "Libby Sartain, Vice President of People, Southwest Airlines," *Training* (January 2001).

Page xiv "And people will stand in line . . ." Lisa Belkin, "Life's Work, If Chocolate Doesn't . . . ," *New York Times* (January 31, 2001), quoting an Integra Realty Resources study.

Page xv "The *Harvard Business Review* estimates . . ." A great article on Presenteeism was published by Keith Dixon, *Chief Executive* (June 2005). It contained the *Harvard Business Review* statistics we quoted.

Page xvi "According to several recent studies, . . ." Del Jones, "Best Friends Good for Business,"

USA Today (November 30, 2004), quoting FranklinCovey and Gallup statistics on employee disengagement.

Page xvi   "According to a 2003 survey, . . ." Recognition and commitment/morale statistics were culled from a survey commissioned by the authors and conducted by Wirthlin Worldwide. Interviews took place from March 6 to 10, 2003, with 1,000 U.S. adults 18 years of age and older. The margin of error was ± 3.1 at 95 percent confidence. Respondents were randomly selected throughout the country to obtain a representative and projectable sample.

Chapter One

Page 6   "Some 88 percent of . . ." "Guess What's Still #1," Kudos, vol. 3, no. 4 (December 1998). Quoting Adele B. Lynn, management consultant, Lynn Learning Labs, HR Fact Finder.

Page 6   "Here's another frightening stat: . . ." Dody Tsiantar, "The Cost of Incivility," Time (February 7, 2005).

Page 6   "Just listen to this: . . ." Shaoni Bhattacharya, "Unfair Bosses Make Blood Pressure Soar," NewScientist.com News Service (June 24, 2003). The article can be found at newscientist.com/news/news.jsp?id=ns99993863.

Page 7   "David Sirota, coauthor of . . ." The
David Sirota interview was published
in this biweekly online resource:
Knowledge@Wharton, from the Whar-
ton School at the University of Pennsylvania on May 4, 2005, under the title,
"Giving Workers What They Want: The
Returns Are Huge." We've quoted the
article several times.

Page 7   "The Global Employee Commitment
Study by Hewitt Associates . . ." The
Gallup Management Journal is a
monthly online resource where you can
access Gallup's semi-annual Employee
Engagement Index, among other gems.
For the statistics we quoted, see Steve
Crabtree, "Getting Personal in the
Workplace," *Gallup Management Journal*
(June 10, 2004).

Page 7   "Backing that up is a . . ." "U.S. Job
Satisfaction Keeps Falling," *The Conference Board* (February 28, 2005).

Page 8   "Said Marcus Buckingham and . . ."
Marcus Buckingham and Curt Coffman,
*First Break All The Rules: What the
World's Greatest Managers Do Differently*
(New York: Simon & Schuster, 1999).

Page 10   "In the Gallup organization's ongoing . . ." Tom Rath, "The Best Ways to
Recognize Employees," *Gallup Management Journal* (December 9, 2004).

Page 13   "Even today, almost every senior . . ."
B. P. Noble, "At Work: The Bottom Line
on People Issues," *New York Times* (February 19, 1995). Quoting a Towers Perrin Study.

Page 13   "As a result, an astounding 65 . . ."
Tom Rath and Donald O. Clifton, PhD,
How Full Is Your Bucket? Positive Strategies for Work and Life (New York: Gallup
Press, 2004).

Page 14   "In response, workers have created . . ."
"U.S. Job Satisfaction Keeps Falling," *The
Conference Board* (February 28, 2005).

Chapter Two

Page 24   "Well, according to the National Society . . ." Society for Human Resource
Management, 1997 Retention Practices
Survey.

Page 24   "Not surprisingly, Prudential Financial . . ." Barbara Parus, "Recognition:
A Strategic Tool for Retaining Talent,"
Workspan (November 2002).

Page 25   "A study by the Saratoga Institute . . ."
American Management Society, Saratoga Institute, *Retention Management:
Strategies, Practices, Trends: A Report*
(New York: AMACOM Books, 1997).

Page 26   "Says Marshall Goldsmith, . . ." Marshall Goldsmith, "Retaining High-Impact
Performers," *Leader to Leader* premiere
issue, found on Marshallgoldsmith.com.

Page 27   "Of them he said, . . ." Candace Wal-
           ters, "Creating an effective performance
           appraisal system," *HR Works.com* (Au-
           gust 31, 2001), quoting Jack Welch's
           last letter to shareholders.

Page 29   "Not long ago, a survey of . . ." "A Case
           for Incentives," *PFI Newsletter* (Novem-
           ber 2002), combining studies from the
           Gallup Organization (2,000 full-time
           employees) and from the International
           Society for Performance Improvement.
           The results showed 39 percent of em-
           ployees with recognition initiatives in
           place were "extremely satisfied" with
           their current company, versus nine per-
           cent for employees at companies without
           such initiatives.

Page 29   "Tom Rath and Donald Clifton in . . ."
           Tom Rath and Donald O. Clifton, PhD,
           *How Full Is Your Bucket? Positive Strate-
           gies for Work and Life* (New York: Gallup
           Press, 2004).

Page 30   "Research supporting the effective-
           ness . . ." Elizabeth B. Hurlock, "An
           Evaluation of Certain Incentives Used in
           School Work," *Journal of Educational Psy-
           chology* (March 16).

Page 32   "Our friend Quint Studer, . . ." Much of
           Quint Studer's excellent work is
           captured in his book *Hardwiring
           Excellence* (Gulf Breeze, FL: Fire
           Starter Publishing, 2003).

Page 33   "Consider the Watson-Wyatt . . ." Watson Wyatt Strategic Rewards Survey 1998, conducted in conjunction with *Employee Benefits Magazine.*

Page 33   "Compare it to recent Hewitt . . ." Pi Wen Looi, Ted Marusarz, and Raymond Baumruk, "What Makes a Best Employer" (Hewitt Talent and Organization Consulting White Paper, 2004).

Page 34   "According to William Bliss, . . ." Clare Fitzgerald, "The Human Factor," *Insight,* the magazine of the Illinois CPA Society (September/October 2004), quoting William Bliss.

Chapter Three

Page 44   "The late Cotton Fitzsimmons, former coach . . ." For sources on Cotton Fitzsimmons, we have quoted Mike Tulumello, "Cotton Was a Man of Character, Principle," *East Valley Tribune* (July 26, 2004); as well as the history section of nba.com at nba.com/history /fitzsmmons_040726.html; and the Moody Church Radio News Website at moodychurch.org/radio/newsletters /Vol2No3.pdf.

Page 46   "Ian Stewart, author of . . ." Ian Stewart, *Does God Play Dice? The Mathematics of Chaos* (Oxford, England and New York: Blackwell, 1989).

Page 47   "*Incentive Magazine* reports that . . ." Maggie Rauch, "Cash and Praise a Powerful Combo," *Incentive Magazine* (June 1, 2003).

Page 56   "Paul Smucker, Former J. M. Smucker and Company CEO, . . ." Peter Economy and Bob Nelson, *Managing for Dummies* (Foster City, CA: IDG Books, 1996), quoting Paul Smucker.

Page 63   "In a Wirthlin Worldwide survey of 1,010 award . . ." *American Express Incentive Services Website FAQ* quoting (March 1999) Wirthlin Worldwide survey of 1,010 people who were asked how they spent their last cash reward. Access this at aeis.com/Incentive _FAQs.html.

Chapter Four

Page 79   " 'Recognition is America's most underused . . ." Jennifer Nii, "Bank Chief Outlines Art of Leading," *Deseret Morning News* (Salt Lake City, UT: October 14, 2004).

Page 87   "According to a survey of more than 33,000 . . ." O. C. Tanner Recognition Company recipient survey in 2004.

Page 100   "Informal or day-to-day awards . . ." Recognition every 7 days was first coined by Marcus Buckingham and Curt Coffman, *First Break All The Rules: What the World's Greatest Managers Do Differently* (New York: Simon & Schuster, 1999).

Page 100 "Dee Hansford, who headed Disney World . . ." More on Dee Hansford's work at Disney can be found in the World@Work publication "The Magic of Employee Recognition 10 Proven Tactics from CalPERS and Disney" (Hansford).

Page 110 "For 365 more ideas . . ." Adrian Gostick and Chester Elton, *A Carrot A Day* (Layton, UT: Gibbs Smith Publisher, 2004).

Chapter Five

Page 117 "Marcus Buckingham, author of . . ." Marcus Buckingham, *The One Thing You Need to Know about Great Managing, Great Leading, and Sustaining Individual Success* (New York: Simon & Schuster, 2005).

Page 118 "According to Hewitt's work . . ." "A Powerful and Engaging New Business Weapon," *Boardroom,* Issue 43, Article 2, interview with Paul Osgood of Hewitt.

Page 118 "In their book, *Giving Employees . . .*" "*Giving Employees What They Want: The Returns Are Huge,*" Knowledge@ Warton (May 4, 2005).

Chapter Six

Page 130 "And he's not alone. . . ." "What Will Keep Employees in Place?" *Sales and Marketing Executive Report* (February 12, 2001), quoting Nierenberg Group and New York University's Management Institute study of 900 professionals across the United States.

Page 134 "Stephen P. Robbins, author of . . ." Stephen P. Robbins, *The Truth about Managing People: And Nothing But the Truth* (London and New York: Financial Times/Prentice Hall, 2003).

Page 134 "In his book, *The Choice . . .*" John C. Maxwell, *The Choice Is Yours* (Nashville, TN: J. Countryman, 2005).

Conclusion

Page 138 "Because 56 million jobs will open . . ." bls.gov/emp is a great site for U.S. employment numbers, including percent change and average annual job openings.

Page 138 "As the founder of the online job . . ." Paul Michelman, "Your New Core Strategy: Employee Retention," *Working Knowledge for Business Leaders Newsletter* (Harvard Business School, November 26, 2003).

ABOUT THE AUTHORS

Adrian Gostick is the author of several success-ful books including: the *Wall Street Journal* and *BusinessWeek* best-seller *A Carrot a Day*; the UPI international best-seller *The Integrity Advantage;* and *The 24-Carrot Manager,* which has been called a "must-read for modern-day managers" by Larry King of CNN. Adrian's books have been translated into 15 languages and have sold hun-dreds of thousands of copies. As an employee mo-tivation expert, he has appeared on ABC and CNBC television, and has written for *USA Today Magazine, HR Executive* and *Investor's Business Daily.* Adrian is managing director of The Carrot Culture Group where he consults with organiza-tions to build effective employee recognition pro-grams. Adrian earned a master's degree in Strategic Communication and Leadership from

Seton Hall University, where he is currently a guest lecturer on organizational culture. He can be reached at adrian@carrots.com.

Chester Elton is coauthor of *Managing with Carrots,* which was nominated as the Society of Human Resource Management (SHRM) Book of the Year. He also coauthored the best-sellers *The 24-Carrot Manager* and *A Carrot a Day.* As a motivation expert, Chester has been featured in the *Wall Street Journal, Washington Post,* and *Fast Company* magazine, has been profiled in the *New York Times,* and was called "an apostle of appreciation" by the *Globe and Mail* (Canada). He has been a guest on CNN, NBC's *Today Show,* and on National Public Radio. A sought-after speaker and recognition consultant, Chester is vice president of performance recognition with the O. C. Tanner Recognition Company. He was the highest rated speaker at the 2005 SHRM annual conference, and has spoken to delighted audiences in Asia, Europe, and throughout North America. He serves as a recognition consultant to Fortune 100 firms such as Johnson & Johnson, AOL/Time Warner, Avis, and KPMG. You can contact him at chester@carrots.com.

Learn more about the authors and the Carrot Culture at **carrots.com** or **invisibleemployee.com**.